Unbound Spirit:

Personal Stories of Transformation

Unbound Spirit:

Personal Stories of Transformation

Edward L. Walsh

Open Wings

Publishing

Open Wings Publishing

Long Beach, California

Unbound Spirit: Personal Stories of Transformation

By Edward L. Walsh

Published by:

Open Wings Publishing

P.O. Box 8020

Long Beach, California 90808

Publisher's- Cataloging-in-Publication
        (Prepared by Dorothy L. Strang, retired librarian)
Walsh, Edward L. 1950-
        Unbound spirit: personal stories of transformation/
        by Edward L. Walsh.
        p.   cm.
Includes bibliographical references and index
ISBN 0-9677977 1-3   : $14.95
LCCN: 00-091032
1. Biography-collective. 2. Philosophy-metaphysics. I. Title
BF1026.W2   2000
158.1W2

Cover and interior design by Marty Bunch

Editing: Marilyn Jensen, James Flaherty

DEDICATION PAGE

I dedicate this book to the contributors. I deeply appreciate your sharing. May the depth and wisdom of your stories touch others as they have astonished, moved and changed me. Thank You.

Honor and celebrate your humanity

CONTENTS

Acknowledgments

I want to extend a special thank you to the following people for their support and assistance with Unbound Spirit: Marty Bunch, Billie Dier, James Flaherty, Marilyn Jensen, Susan Oushani, and Kerry Tillman.

I also want to thank the following authors and publishers for allowing me to reprint parts of the following books:

Joy's Way by Brugh Joy, copyright 1979 by Brugh Joy. Used by permission of Jeremy P. Tarcher, a division of Penguin Putnam Inc.

In Tune with the Infinite by Ralph Waldo Trine, copyright by Ralph Waldo Trine. Used by permission of Kessinger Publishing Co. P.O. Box 160, Kila, Mt. 59920

Introduction

Unbound Spirit: Personal Stories of Transformation came alive in the early 1980's shortly after I read Sun Bear's book *Path of Power*, which describes the American Indian tradition of vision quests. With a lot of enthusiasm and plenty of sublime ignorance, I decided to venture out in the desert near Joshua Tree National Monument in search of a vision. I chronicled that experience with its revealed wisdom for the Widesky Men's Council and Orange County Jung Club's newsletters. I was pleasantly surprised with the response to the article, and I have included it as the first story of the book.

About 1995, I took a weekend workshop with Brugh Joy. He invited a few participants to share their personal accounts of life events that they felt were spiritually significant. Although the stories were short and concise, they all contained a numinous quality that was very enriching. Hearing these stories touched a deep place within me, as their wisdom, humility and peace resonated through me.

During the next few days, I began to think about how a book of spirit-filled experiential stories would inspire others as those in the workshop had moved me. I already knew the impact of my vision quest on myself and those who had responded to my article. With some trepidation, I bravely took the initial steps to begin the process of collecting transformational stories. Collecting these stories was accomplished through an in depth audio tape interview. While conducting the interview, I generally allowed each person to tell his or her story from their own perspective, only asking questions to elucidate the events or set the frame for the experience. A few of the stories required research, which allowed me to better understand and write the material relevant to the story.

After writing the first story in third person, I quickly realized that to capture the personal feeling and immediacy of these stories required that I write them in first person. Although I authored each of the stories, I used the interview transcripts as often as possible and submitted each finished manuscript for revision by each person whose story is included in the book. Some required many revisions while others were accepted as I had written them. Still, one characteristic was common and compelling – these people were committed to their stories and to the unfolding meaning which touched and reshaped their lives.

Each story has reshaped my life by expanding and opening my overall perspective. Each one conveys a feeling of being alive in a way that transcends time and space. For me, the effect was to make it feel as if they were happening to me even though the actual experiences were not mine.

There is a numinous quality to these stories that goes beyond the barriers of time and space. They create an opening into an "other worldliness" that is captivating. We know that, in our everyday lives, we must attend to the realities of time and space; there are those times when we experience coincidence or actual glimpses into realities where life's fragmentations, such as with time and space, evaporate and are synthesized into a new order.

Another change in my view of life came in 1998 when I went to Hawaii to interview Brugh Joy and Serge King. Due to a change in my itinerary, I stayed in Maui for two days before going to Kauai for the interviews. I decided to revisit the Seven Sacred Pools on the Hana side of the island. Some years earlier, I had unsuccessfully attempted to hike the two mile trail that leads inland through the verdant jungle to a gigantic waterfall. In crossing the stream that flows from the waterfall, I cut my hand when I fell on some slippery rocks. The rocks were treacherous, so I decided that the better part of valor was to keep the rest of my body intact. So I headed back towards the trailhead and the coastline leaving the waterfall and the remaining one and three-fourths miles of trail for another day.

This time I was determined to reach the waterfall even if I had to crawl across that stream. To my surprise and relief, a foot bridge had been built over the stream and the precarious slippery rocks. I felt this auspiciously signaled that my determination was not to be quailed. Unknown to me at the time, I was headed for an experience that would give me a deeper appreciation for my human fear.

The trail led through the jungle into a bamboo forest, whose round thin stalks towered twenty to thirty feet above the ground. At times, the bamboo was so thick, I felt as though I was walking through a tunnel. The effect of the density, height and shape of the bamboo engendered a feeling of awe towards this living sculpture. On and off, rain drops sprinkled down into this dark, damp passageway creating a unique sound, texture, and ambiance.

Once through the bamboo forest, I was greeted with filtered light as the sun poked through the clouds and jungle. For most of the remaining one-half mile trek to the waterfall, the sun was again completely shining forth its brilliance, which is so typical of the Hawaiian rain-sunshine dance. Although Hana had been experiencing a drought, there was still plenty of water cascading down the several hundred feet of rock face to generate a glorious sight of dancing and floating liquid-light globules. While viewing this magnificent water show, I felt compelled to speak about the mysterious bamboo forest with an anonymous hiker standing nearby. "How did you like the bamboo forest?" I asked. He said nothing.

On the way to the waterfall, I was passed by a group of teenagers walking much faster than I was. On my journey back to the coastline I said "hi" to a young couple heading towards the waterfall, telling them it was magnificent. As I

entered the bamboo forest, I was again awed by the unique-
ness of the long poles and their density. Just then a rain cloud
came overhead, pouring down drops of water which created a
"rat-a-tat-tat" drumming sound as it beat against the bamboo.
This fast moving cloud and the rain shower darkened the
shadowy-lit nature of this living enclosure even more. For
one quick moment, a distortion shifted the scene directly
ahead of me, then just as quickly as it came the cloud passed
overhead with an accompanying lift in the heaviness of the
shadowed darkness. I happily continued to hike forward as I
enjoyed the dripping sounds of water against bamboo.

Not too much time had passed when I came face to face
with the same group of teenagers that had passed me earlier
on the trail going to the waterfall. Since I had headed back
before they did, I assumed that they had taken a trail-loop that
was much faster. When I asked them if that's what they had
done, they looked at me as though I was talking a foreign
language. I felt a little taken aback with their non-respon-
siveness.

Continuing on ahead, I came across two stragglers from
the same group of teenagers, and I asked if they had taken a
trail-loop. Again I receive the same response which baffled
me. When I originally greeted them on the way to the waterfall, they seemed friendly. Now their lack of verbal response
puzzled me.

Once through the bamboo, the sunlight pierced through
the jungle in patches of shadow and light, but the trail somehow didn't seem right. I continued to walk along expecting to
see the footbridge soon. Instead, I came to a small stream
where the trail crossed to some rocks which were about five
feet above the stream on the other side. I felt confused.
Crossing the stream, I looked up at the rocks and saw the
waterfall behind them. I was stunned, my mind whirling. In
just a few seconds, the young couple who had passed me on
their way to the waterfall came walking toward me on the

trail. They paused, smiled, and said, "Oh, you decided to come back to the waterfall."

I can't imagine what my expression looked like, but not a word came out of my mouth in response. As they proceeded ahead, they looked bewildered. Immediately, a feeling of terror ran through my body as the thought of being trapped forever in this jungle quickly spun through my mind.

I made a quick decision to follow the couple who were now reentering the jungle and were almost out of my sight. The last thing I wanted to do was walk alone! I imagined myself caught in some Twilight Zone vortex loop which would spin me around for eternity. As I entered the jungle, again trying to catch the couple ahead of me, I heard a chuckling laughter that was inaudible to my ears but seemed to be all around me, permeating everything. Somehow, I realized I was connected and in communication with an energetic entity and it was laughing at me. Through this empathic link, I immediately knew what had happened. I had been the butt of a joke and in some way had been completely turned around with an energy created by the fast moving clouds and resonating sound of the rain on bamboo. I remembered the shift in my perception, like a wobble on a television screen.

As I raced along trying to catch the couple ahead of me, I was still afraid – what else might happen to me. And yet another emotion – anger – was beginning to build within me. Still linked to this "other," my wrath turned into a discourse of complaints at the unfair nature of this prank. "Can't you see that I can only walk so far?" "This is inexcusable, with my disability I had walked my limit and now I'm forced to walked more." "How could you?" I even began complaining to the trees that I was a good person, and as I bent down to pick up a piece of trash, I became even more righteous. On and on I continued, until a rather old wise-looking tree responded by firmly telling me to get off it. Yes, believe it or not I was able to hear this tree.

The experience of being tricked and laughed at had touched a painful place within me, triggering an anger I used to cover up and hide my terror. Through my telepathic link, I knew the enormous size of this entity or energy. I was trying to pretend with my righteous anger that had I been unjustly abused, but it was my fear of this unknown "other" that took the fun out of this jolly playful prank.

I now feel somewhat safe in the belief that I would not be harmed if I returned to hike the trail to that spectacular waterfall. Still, I have regrets regarding my reaction. Why does fear habitually dominated life? Will I ever experience novel circumstances without fear? Such questions are addressed through the personal stories and the book's philosophical self-help chapters.

Life's mysteries seem to be beyond complete knowledge. Much of humanity's pursuit to understand life and our environment has been beneficial, helping society deal more effectively with necessities of living. Still, this very quest to define life has often blocked the very portals by which we can perceive and experience more of the unseen essence behind all existence. Caught in our own daily expectations, the doors of our conscious perception are shut and locked around us, creating a house of mirrors and excluding the opportunity to glean more of life's mystery. To know – to have knowledge makes us feel safe and important. It creates the ground and context of our lives. To be open, to let go of all images and image making requires that we move to a true experience of faith, a true experience of the unity of all.

Take this journey. Sail with your own unfettered spirit as do all true adventurers. Let your soul's wind chart your course to self-discovery by reading these personal stories with an open heart. See, perhaps for the first time, the un-limited ability of our "unbound spirit" to enter our lives with the joy and amazement that self-expansion and true freedom brings.

Ed Walsh

Author's note: After my two-day layover in Maui, I flew to Kauai to interview Brugh Joy and Serge King. I asked them both about my experience hiking back from the water-fall and inland from the Seven Sacred Pools. Brugh said, there are many autonomous energies on the island while Serge King said, everything is autonomous and contains life. From my point of view, they are both correct with autonomy being measured in degrees of conscious freedom.

Transforming Stories

Storytelling is a staple of life. When we listen to the news, read the Bible, or hear a fairytale, we are involved in story. Story passes on the wisdom and Spirit of one generation to the next, helping humanity to evolve. In *The Man Who Wrestled With God*, John Sanford tells about Lauren van der Post, an explorer and author, who once lived with the Bushmen of Kalahari Desert. While with the tribe, van der Post tried for several months to get them to relate their folktale and tribal stories, but the Bushmen only denied that such stories existed. Only after they began to trust him did they tell their origin of the world, first man and how animals were created stories. Holding the spirit of their existence, their stories were of primary import and needed to be protected.

As I look back over my many years of questing for self understanding and development, I realize that there are experiences that quicken and move me in a heightened way. These experiences seem to be timeless, bringing a feeling of the Spirit regardless of when I recall them. Surrendering of my ego-personality to this greater spiritual force is a necessary ingredient to these experiential stories. These stories can be transformative and range from being a wake-up call to a simple demonstration of self-folly.

In the mid-1980's, I read Sun Bear's book, *The Path of Power*. He told about how vision quests were done within the American Indian tradition. A vision quest is a ritual time and place where an individual seeks a spiritual vision and path. I was very moved by the idea of a vision quest and decided to attempt one on my own.

Although the book indicated that vision quests could last for days and even weeks, I decided that I could modify the time required. I arranged for a room at a metaphysical retreat center near Joshua Tree National Park. I decided to fast the day before and to drive there early in the morning without much sleep so that I would arrive sometime prior to sunrise.

My plan was going smoothly as I arrived at the retreat center just about two hours before sunrise. I had prearranged to meet my host in front of my room at 10:00 a.m. to pay him. It was dark and I was alone. I decided to walk out in the desert. Perhaps in hindsight that was not such a wise idea but facing my fears and moving through them was an important part of the quest. I walked for several hours and I was indeed scared. Joshua trees appeared like malevolent creatures. At just prior to dawn, I was walking on the ridge of a hill. I looked down at this rock. As in a psychedelic movie, it began to vibrate and seemed to be in motion and felt alive. I refocused my eyes and it was again still but my feeling for inanimate objects was forever changed. As dawn broke, I heard a dog barking. I concentrated on this yelping sound, trying to locate where it was coming from. It seemed to come from the core of the hill in front of me. My mind flashed on the image of the Pied Piper when he opened the mountain and the children went within. I felt like I could see inside the hill which was an infinite black still void. These experiences were tantalizing, but the vision I sought was not forthcoming.

I was tired. I decided to return to my room and wait to pay my host. To my amazement the man was waiting there for me. This surprised me because I felt that I was early. Perhaps I was early but at that time in the morning and the state I was experiencing, everything had an unusual feeling to it.

After paying my bill and thanking the man I took my things into the room. I was hungry, tired and frustrated. I felt my efforts were in vain, and I truly felt underwhelmed. Having received no vision, I ate lightly and went to sleep. I had a dream. A man in his late fifties to early sixties who was solidly built with a bald head appeared to me. Looking up at him, I heard him say in a matter-of-fact voice "Who are you doing this for?" I woke up startled.

Who are you doing this for? This question is obviously funny, clearly pointing out my self-involvement and folly. But this question is more important to me and, I think, to life than the lack of my development. The question haunts me to this day with its mana – its spirit! In the heart of this question is the suggestion of the great split between man and God and perhaps a way to bridge this gap.

Most mystics do not describe a split between man and God but describe a oneness, a wholeness or an essential unity to which we all belong. Considering the diversity of life, it is difficult to imagine that somehow life is all tied together. This is especially true when our views differ from one another as they so often do. But if the mystics are correct that we all are part of some greater wholeness, then I feel the question "Who are you doing this for?" becomes a significant touchstone in our lives.

Using this question daily can help us to check our motives and evaluate the differences between individual, community and collective ways that a person can act. For example, giving to those in "need" certainly helps my community and connects me to our greater wholeness, but takes away some of my individual resources. This decision to forego one aspect of myself for another can be either consciously or unconsciously done. The ability to dance consciously between the different aspects of ourselves helps to

determine our maturational development. It gives us choice
relevant to a given circumstance and moment. If, for
example, we are always acting just our of our individual
needs, we eliminate our connection to others – both
spiritually and within community. Another example would
be someone living just out of his spiritual aspect, as in some
religious orders, leaving their individual and community
development to wane and to atrophy. The mature person is
able to hold the tension consciously between all his or her
parts while acting in the moment. Buddhists call this right
action.

Personally, I have asked myself what was I searching for
out in that desert. Looking back I wish my question would
have been a conscious one. The truth is that my dream-ques-
tion illuminated my personal development too clearly. I was
seeking my Promethian light of self-gain and personal
power like so many who begin their spiritual journey. The
quest for guidance and direction for my place in the great
Jig Saw Puzzle was truly lacking.

"Who are you doing this for?" does not exclude the importance of personal individuation and growth. Having been
raised in an alcoholic family, I am well aware of this fact.
Shame, criticism, violence and the threat of violence solidify
into low self-esteem. The family need for survival requires
that individual development be sacrificed to protect the
whole. People-pleasing, control and codependency are the
glue of survival. In this type of family, "Who are you doing
this for?" was not addressed, except as an unconscious need
for the clan to survive.

On a spiritual journey the same question begins to take on
a new meaning. Again I am placed in contrast with another
but the other in this case is not human. Now I am called to
see myself in juxtaposition to a greater dimension. In a

spiritual reality, "Who am I doing this for?" calls me to be clear between what I am on the personality level and how what I am contributes to or diminishes my individuality, my community and spirit at large – how my actions or inaction can affect the whole, everyone and everything.

This is a question for daily living, asking us to reflect on our motives and to aim for a higher purpose. To see and to realize that together we all can win in our individual quest for wholeness. When we can answer this question often enough with integrity and honesty, we can move in our lives with the sight and glide of an eagle.

Ray's Story
Self-Made Man

That day, like so many, was a hard day. The nuns were on me about how I wasn't working up to my potential. In fact, I received a "c" instead of an "a" on one of my science reports to nail home the point. I walked home alone because I didn't have any real friends. When I walked into the living room, there was my dad sprawled on the hardwood floor, a pool of vomit around his head. I slowly walked over to him and lightly kicked the bottle. I heard a ring when it hit the floor but it didn't break. I cleaned up my dad's face and the floor; then, somehow I managed to get him up onto the couch. I went up to my room and stared out the window.

As a boy, my family life was very hard. My mother was controlling and my father was an alcoholic. My mother and sister expected me to take care of him when he was drinking, because I was the only one who could. When my mother needed the car keys or some money, she always would send me to dig them out of his pockets.

My father was a periodic alcoholic, so there were plenty of times when he was sober. During those times he wouldn't have anything to do with me, which made me feel lousy and inadequate, as if there was something wrong with me. When I was ten years old, he committed suicide from an overdose of sleeping pills. I felt devastated and numb. My pain and confusion were enormous.

Gambling was my thing. I was good at it, and I started hanging around with some older guys. They drank a lot while playing cards, and at 13, I did my first drinking. It was great; it was an elixir that made me feel good and took away my pain. I continued to use alcohol in ever increasing amounts until my drinking episodes usually resulted in blackouts and oblivion. So often, I would wake up on a slab of cement, the smell of barf and urine everywhere, and realize I was back in the jail drunk tank again. So often drunk, in jail, and/or sick with a hangover, I was a continuous thorn in the side of both my family and employer.

Being in trouble wasn't what I really wanted. I tried to get sober in a number of ways to calm my family and boss. I even tried Alcoholics Anonymous, but in the fifties I saw no young alcoholics like me attending meetings, which made it hard for me to relate. What could a bunch of old farts have to tell me anyway? Besides, I had made a pact with myself since my father's death. I was going to take care of myself. I wasn't going to be controlled or ask for help from anyone. I was going to make it on my own.

Between my early to late teenage years, my drinking got more and more out of control. It was all I could do to stay sober beyond a week or two. Being drunk was like waking up or going to sleep; I knew it was going to happen. I would try to quit and then find myself inexplicably and helplessly drunk, my blackouts becoming longer, the physical pain un-bearable.

My life in Long Beach was definitely at a low. I had no job, and my family didn't want much to do with me. A drinking pal and I decided to go to Las Vegas to find a job. There was nothing unusual about this; it was just one of many wild schemes.

Before leaving we parcel posted our clothes to Las Ve-gas. As with most of our crazy exploits, we were drinking heavily and I had finished off five quarts of wine when we were finally picked up by a guy in a little '41 Coupe going all the way to Las Vegas.

As we got in the car Billy said, "Thanks mister. How far you headed?"

"I'm going all the way to Las Vegas," said the driver.

"That's great," said Billy.

"What's wrong with your friend? He looks like he seen a ghost. How come he's shakin' up a storm?"

"Oh, Ray? He's just a little under the weather."

There was room enough for just the three of us. I was going into the delirium tremens, D.T.'s. I had the shakes, insomnia, and couldn't eat or drink anything without the dry heaves. My thinking was certainly distorted. Normal sounds were driving me crazy.

After about an hour or so I said to the driver, "Stop the car! Let me out here! This is my uncle's farm!" Actually, I had no idea where we were. I certainly didn't have an uncle who was a farmer. I just couldn't take being stuck between two people in that cramped car. It was driving me crazy.

The driver looked at me as if I were nuts; he let us out somewhere in the middle of orange groves in Riverside, California. Somehow, we made it close to the main line of the railroads that travel through the Cajon Pass near San Bernardino. The trains were mandated to blow their horns all the way through the crossing. After about an hour, I could predict when the first blast of the horn would go off. The sound was so devastating that I felt like my insides were coming out. I'd hold myself in a fetal position with my hands over my ears, and still the sound was torture.

The torture from those horns went on most of the day before we got another ride. In those days, there were no freeways, and traveling took more time. It was several hours later before we got that ride going into Las Vegas. Without knowing how, I found myself on the Las Vegas courthouse lawn, so sick I could hardly move. Billy had vanished, probably searching out some bar or liquor store.

Lying there, feeling weak and sick, unable to walk or crawl, I felt devastated. I had no friends, nowhere to go, and no money. I was very tired. I had been getting drunk, quitting, and getting drunk again in an endless cycle. I hadn't been thinking clearly for several months. Years later, I learned I had been suffering from Organic Brain Syndrome. This is where you beat the brain up so much with alcohol that memory, concentration, reasoning, and various physical functions are severely debilitated. On that lonely day, I was beaten physically, emotionally, and spiritually.

And then, in this depth of my misery and confusion, something miraculous happened. A clarity of thought came upon me that had an objective feeling to it, like I was outside myself. Clarity was in direct contrast to the confusion and physical pain that I had been experiencing. This overwhelmed me.

As I lay there a lucid thought came to me with the force and brilliance of a lightning flash: *Well, you finally made it – you're a self-made man!* Right then I knew the bitter truth of my life. The physical pain was nothing compared to the mental and emotional war going on in my head. My life was valueless and spiritually devoid. I felt the bitter cold loneliness of a man who had pushed everyone away. I could truly see how doing it all on my own without help from anyone had made me a self-made man.

This lucid thinking amazed me. I shouldn't be able to do this. My mind and body were shot, and here I was thinking objectively with great awareness. It felt something like a near-death experience where the person is looking down at their own body seeing all that's going on.

And then came the thought: Are you really willing to stop? I was desperately tired. I wanted to quit! Amazingly, I now knew I had a choice. Except for very early in my drinking, I had never had a choice. I just found myself helplessly drunk again. Now, I had a real feeling of choice: I could continue on with alcohol until my body gave way and then die, or I could seek help.

I felt no compulsion to do the right thing; I really felt I had a choice and with this lucid thinking, I questioned myself: Am I really willing to go to any length to get sober? I hadn't been in the past. Then I thought of the most degrading thing I would have to do to get sober: I imagined myself standing on 6th and Main in downtown Los Angeles, dressed in a white robe and sandals selling Bible tracts. Embarrassing as this might be, I was still willing to do anything.

I made it to the A.A.meeting two and a half blocks away. There I stopped making excuses about my age. I honestly thought I don't care if it's a 90-year-old black woman, if she used to drink and she doesn't drink anymore, I wanted to know how she did it. My acceptance problem was now gone. I figured that we all had the same disease. Like diabetes, it didn't matter whether we're 19 or 50; we were going through the same experiences and had similar characteristics. Now, solving alcoholism was our common denominator.

I went to that meeting with an open mind and a clarity of thought. For the first time, I listened with the intent of hearing how the people of A.A. solve their problems. I shared my situation. I didn't ask for anything except for help in becoming sober.

After the meeting a deputy sheriff from Clark County offered to help me. He needed some help painting and fixing up a homestead house. He took me to his house the next day, but I was so physically sick I couldn't do anything for a couple days. After several days working at his house, I accompanied him into town, where he had business and errands.

I was determined to get a job that day. I just started walking down one side of Fremont Street asking every business if they needed some help. I eventually got a job in a gas station. It wasn't a great job, but it allowed me to save enough money to get back to Long Beach.

When I returned to Long Beach, I continued to attend A.A. meetings and have been doing so for forty years. I sponsor newcomers, and my wife and I host an Adult Children of Alcoholics meeting once a week in my home. Forty years plus since my experience in Las Vegas and with the help of the A.A. membership, the program, and the grace of God, I've stayed sober.

I'll never forget the miracle that happened to me on the courthouse lawn in Las Vegas. On that miraculous day, my life was changed.

Chris's Story

God's Grace

"I pronounce you man and wife."

It was one of the happiest days of my life. Rebecca and I had been dating for about a year, ever since we had met on a mission trip for our respective churches. We both felt like we had been called into a relationship and marriage was the natural next step. At the end of August, 1975 we married, and eight days later we piled most of our possessions into a truck and headed off to Princeton where I had been accepted as a master's candidate in ministerial divinity. We had a wonderful trip across the country and arrived with little more than a dollar in our pockets. She was 18, I was 23 and we were both ready for our new life's adventure.

Rebecca right away began to feel isolated. It was her first significant time away from family and friends and since we couldn't afford for her to attend college, developing friends was more difficult in this unfamiliar town. My long hours studying, attending school and working didn't give us much quality time. We both had to work just to barely make ends meet. With strong efforts on both our parts, I graduated and was called to a small church in San Juan Capistrano.

Life was much better back in Southern California. We were back home among friends, and we were both very active in the church. Although we had nothing to compare it to, we both felt our relationship and marriage were good, with our first child being angel sent from God.

Although things were good, I still wanted more of a challenge and felt dissatisfied with my current position. I

wanted to stretch and grow in my career, and so I started exploring alternatives.

I interviewed with a church in Pittsburgh, Pennsylvania.
They really liked us. They pulled out all the stops, wined and
dined us, and offered me an incredible salary. We took the
job and again moved eastward, leaving family and friends for
what we thought was an ideal opportunity. It meant we could
get above water financially, and I could take on more responsibility with new opportunities to serve in my chosen calling.

Our relationship began slipping right away for a variety
of reasons. The job was demanding, and I followed the mind-
set of the many executives in our community who worked
seventy to eighty hours a week. As with Princeton, Rebecca
had trouble making friends, and events like the University
Women's group withdrawing their invitation to join their organization didn't help. To be excluded because she didn't
have the necessary college degree was very hurtful and humiliating.

Within our first year in Pittsburgh, our second child was
born which added greatly to our stress. Tyler never slept
more than 20 minutes and was always screaming and could
not be comforted – the fact that Rebecca could not nurse
added to her frustration, discomfort and lack of self-accep-
tance.

Rebecca's life began to shrink into our dark bedroom
where she spent most of her time. We both went to a pedia-
trician and several other medical doctors trying to help Tyler
and relieve some of our stress. I helped out by only working
two nights a week. This allowed me to help with the kids and
other chores around the house. After a year Tyler snapped out
of it, and things seemed to begin to turn around.

We bought a house in a nice neighborhood and started fixing it up. We redid the kitchen, put on a new roof, and added a deck which totally transformed the house. Rebecca started getting out of the house by selling Jafra cosmetics; we made it a family thing. We went to sales meetings together and I even made deliveries. There were some great successes in the church ministry, and we even took a European tour. Life seemed better.

Still, Rebecca wasn't satisfied; she felt that there was something missing in our relationship. We decided to see a marriage counselor and right away began working on com- munication issues. Rebecca had a hard time defining what was wrong; it was something she couldn't put her finger on and I had a hard time expressing my feelings. One of the major problems was my job hours, so I cut them down to 50 hours a week which is a very light work load for a minister. With the counseling help, our relationship seemed to get better. The counselor told us that we were doing well and to go on and enjoy our lives – that we were where we wanted to be.

Shortly, after we stopped the counseling, Rebecca said that she wanted to go see a mutual friend of ours who hap- pened to be her old boyfriend. She came back really changed! She said, "I found a spark, a vitality and a feeling of being alive again." She was emphatic that our relationship was not working and then revealed that in addition to the counselor we were seeing, she had been seeing another counselor who advised her to leave me.

I was devastated! I couldn't believe it.

On Father's Day of 1985, Rebecca brought me a list of things she was taking including our two children, and told me she was leaving in 20 days. I was totally in shock. I'd been under the assumption that with both of our efforts in counseling our relationship had solidified, but I was obviously not in tune with what was going on with Rebecca. Twenty days later she left.

I was a basket case. My heart and passion went out of my job. The church was really hurting for me because they saw my intense pain from the loss of my wife and children who I deeply loved. They generously offered to continue my full salary for six months, so I could look for another job near my children. So I returned to California where I could spend a lot of time with the children while looking for another job. My children were very important to me – I was still their father.

No church would touch me. They didn't want someone in the middle of a divorce, separate from his wife. I had been in the church long enough to know that a selection committee wasn't going to hire a pastor who might leave in six months to follow his children. Nonetheless, I was angry and frustrated that they were not willing to even get to know me. I had a lot to offer a church community.

The next nine months was a real struggle. I was forced back into managing a retail sporting goods store for hardly any money. I was responsible for all the bills: mortgage payment on our home in Pennsylvania, child support payments, etc. My salary barely covered these expenses. I lived a very tenuous existence living out of a room and some boxes – putting gas in the car was often a challenge. When the children stayed over, they slept in sleeping bags next to my bed.

There were times when my emotions were so charged that I was driven to my knees. Even so, I am truly amazed that I never felt abandoned or alone in my struggles as have so many people I have personally known or helped within the scope of my duties. My conviction and experiences of spirit in my life was a wisdom and grace I didn't fully comprehend considering the depth of my pain and self-doubt.

I began to communicate with God as a friend in my daily practical matters. Whenever I was frustrated with one of my employees, I would take long walks on the beach communicating with God. I remember one such employee. I had given her every chance in the world and still she kept acting out in ways that were destructive to the business. I needed to fire her and she really needed the job. On my long walks on the beach, I would dialogue with God asking for direction. I always got feedback that primarily raised two issues: The need for love and forgiveness for the person I was concerned about and a reminder of my own flaws and shortcomings. At the end of each dialogue with God, I always had a feeling of awe, a sense of grace.

When I came to California and started taking walks on the beach, the image of my friend, John, yelling at the ocean would come to mind. John, a graduate of Julliard, was both talented and a bit eccentric. He told me that whenever he felt frustrated with the demands of Julliard, he would go down to the shore and, while facing the ocean, walk knee deep into the water. Then he would scream and yell until he felt a release of tension. After that he would begin to sing, working on his voice and intonation and stayed until he felt better.

It was early in the morning the first time I went to the beach. I was very distraught, and no one seemed to be around. So I just walked into the water about knee deep and started – not knowing who I was yelling at. Embarrassed, I looked around to see if anyone was watching wondering who I was yelling at. I knew that I wasn't yelling at God – He didn't have anything to do with my circumstances. I was already down enough – certainly I wasn't yelling at myself. So I started to focus my yelling at my soon to be ex-wife and found it to be very therapeutic. Then I thought, hey, you don't need to be yelling at her – she's already having a tough enough time.

So I just stopped and I was quiet. In the midst of the silence came an overwhelming sense of peace. I realized that it was the cacophony of noise made by my human mind that symbolized all that was wrong. With the waves and ocean currents pushing and pulling against my legs came the overwhelming sense of the awesome presence of God. My problems felt insignificant – like they were bathed in an inner warmth and sense of peace, scooped up and taken away. It's hard to articulate what happened. It felt like both an outer and inner experience; something like covers being lifted. All I can say for sure is I walked away from the beach with a smile on my face, and I hadn't smiled in a long time.

There was more to this experience than just changing my mood from distraught to joyfully happy. There was now a significant inner change in me. I now had a new sense of presence, wholeness and well-being I didn't have before. This change was either put into me, uncovered, or both. It was as if a curtain had been drawn back on an inner resource – as if something had come over me and at the same time released an inner quality. Now, when I feel overwhelmed, scared, tense, or out of control, I can at will become very much at peace. Not a whole lot can knock me off my feet in the midst of this inner peaceful reality. When I try to describe this inner feeling, along with the words peaceful and serene, the word powerful comes to mind, but it is not the same as human power such as military, political or atomic. John Wesley speaks of this power which comes close to how I feel. He talks about a strange warmth that comes into ones heart.

I found that I have to be vulnerable and humble in the sense of yielding my self-will to tap into this inner state of peace and serenity. I have to let go of the cacophony of voices and noises that run my everyday mind and world. I have to let go of my human manipulations and desires that

are either over or against others and in the midst of any
struggle or tension, I'm at rest, just being...just being.
This state of peace and being has certainly helped me in
my work with others. As a preacher, I am able to transmit
God's Word from a place of conviction and serenity while
sharing myself with openness and honesty. More and more, I
open to God – listening in prayer and meditation – exploring
my emotions, my feelings and my life. Searching for direction in both my failures and accomplishments.

Eric's Story
Wings of a God

"Look Judy, come in here and talk to me. I want to know what's going on," said Eric.

"Leave me alone."

"Come on, I just want to talk to you and find out what's going on."

"If you don't leave me alone, I'm going to pack my bags and leave right now."

"Look, what's going on, talk to me."

I had forced her hand. She got up, packed her bag and left down the stairs. Still, she had been just lying there without saying a word, which was driving me crazy.

How could this be happening? Things between us had been so right earlier that Christmas day. Over the phone, she had even talked to my grandmother in Polish. Hearing them laugh together had made me feel so close to Judy. We were alike in so many ways: the same heritage, the same education, and the same future careers.

She was my magical woman, and I wanted us to build a life together. From the moment I saw her, I was attracted and couldn't keep my eyes off of her. We met at a preparation workshop for our licensing exam, and not long after I had introduced myself, we agreed to study together. We started seeing each other on a regular basis and quickly became very close – the love that grew between us seemed unbelievable.

We had some differences between us, but what couple doesn't. Although we were both raised Catholic, she was very involved in a metaphysical school in Thousand Oaks,

California, and very spiritually oriented. I was studying existential atheism and was far removed from my own spirituality. In fact, my Catholic upbringing was very difficult for me. As a child I was always more of a free spirit, and the nuns in those days went by the maxim spare the rod, spoil the child.

Despite my atheism, during the holidays, I went to considerable trouble to create a beautiful and spiritual Christmas day. With special glazed clay religious ornaments sent by my family, I decorated a Christmas tree. I prepared a Polish Christmas dinner with blessed bread, also family-sent; everything I could think of to build a bridge over those rough spots in our relationship. I had even begun listening to her when she said I was drinking too much. So how could this be happening?

I stared at the tree with my jaw clenched, as my body grew tense and hot. What was going on? Was it over? All my years of pent-up rage I felt toward nuns and Catholicism was directed toward that Christmas tree. In a flash I was at the tree ripping, tearing, stomping and breaking the ornaments. I totally demolished it. Then, it was everything in my house, and finally it was just my house. I ended up groveling on the floor near the tree fading in and out of reality with broken religious ornaments strewn all around me.

As I lay on the floor, I knew the ecstatic joy of Christmas Eve was over. Judy and our dance of closeness was gone, leaving my world in turmoil and rubble. I fingered some of the broken ornaments in a feeble attempt to make them whole again. The broken symbols of my Catholic upbringing overwhelmed me as I faded into a deep place within myself and began reliving vivid images of my youth.

In the world of my childhood, I had imagined Jesus as my companion and friend. Although only make-believe, our play together was full of joy and love that was truly indescribable. It was an emotionally-packed experience then, and as I now relived it. Fading back to reality I saw the broken pieces of glass, the smashed manger, and the Jesus figure in smithereens. These ornamental symbols of love were now totally destroyed. I sobbed uncontrollably, the tears streaming down my face. I remembered the time I had brought my mother flowers with the trust, love, and innocence of my young age. She was angry at me for something I had done to my brother and sent me to my room. I was so furious I ripped the flowers to shreds.

Lying among the broken ornaments and recalling the image of shredded flowers, I knew again the feeling of destroying the things I love in a rageful tantrum. A deep pain filled my chest. I cried out in agony. Everything was smashed and in rubble. For hours, I lay there on Christmas day in a catatonic state, not knowing where I was or what had actually happened.

In my emotional state, taking the next week off work was essential. There was no way I could work while being buffeted by such strong feelings. In an attempt to figure out what had happened, I started a journal, writing down every word that Judy had said, analytically trying to figure out what had happened. I wrote for hours, cried, and wrote some more. For me, making some sense of these experiences was paramount.

During two prior semesters at the university, we had studied and written down our dreams, and now in my desperate search for answers, I began to work with them again. My overwhelming emotions fueled vivid dreams. Combined with the journaling about Judy, I was now engrossed in the symbols of my unconscious. On New Year's Eve, after more than a week of isolation and self-examination, I had a dream that was very similar to my experience I'd had while experimenting with drugs in the late sixties.

In the dream I was running with someone through Boston near where I lived. There was a dream image of a building I saw during an actual drug experience at the age of 18. The building had these old 40-foot doors, and in both the dream and the drug experience I felt awed and a little disoriented by them. I wanted to know who the hell lived in this building with these giant doors. I continued to run down Beacon Street. On the right hand side were Navy barracks. I saw several sailors there and one muscular sailor gave me an intense look. He started to chase me down Beacon Street; he was right behind me as I tried to get away. Running by the Paul Revere house and other historical landmarks, I made it to the Boston Common where a group of people was gathered. A man with a lantern was running through the street saying, "God is dead! God is dead!" As I was running, I began saying, "God is dead! God is dead!" As the group of people watched, the sailor chased me and pulled me down. This look-alike sailor wrestled with me as the crowds applauded and yelled, "Get 'em! Kill 'em!"

I didn't know who they were rooting for, but they were obviously enjoying the fight and wanted more violence. Then a pall came over the crowd, everyone became quiet. As I looked up from the fight with my "twin," I saw a God-like warrior with wings on his head like Mercury; he looked directly at me with a nonverbal expression that said *run with me.* Now I was awed that out of everyone, he signaled me to run with him. I got up and ran with him; he led me through Boston and along the Charles River. Running alongside this God, I felt his energy expand and open me; I felt as though I could run forever. It was a blissful feeling, like this God was calling me and only me for some adventure.

After running with me throughout Boston, past many of the same historical landmarks, he looked at me and said, "Now you'll continue on your own." I had mixed feelings of joy and loss as he ran off and vanished from my sight. Then I saw a line of people waiting to enter a temple or monastery. They were priests but not Christians. First they came in orange robes with staffs, and then people of every kind: different garments, different denominations and different skin colors. I waited, the last in line, and I was aware of peace and tranquillity, a seat, a place for everyone. I walked up and down the rows and aisles looking for a seat, but the temple was full, every spot taken. I started up a stairwell to the belfry; but again, there was not room....people were sitting all the way up. At the very top was an old rotten part of the building where the boards were rickety and unstable, not nailed down adequately.

I looked over, and there was this woman with whom I work, at my real world job. She said, "What are you going to do now, Eric?" I felt this question go right through my heart, deep into my core. On the edge of the tower, the only place available, I sat down on this beam. The nails snapped, the board sank, almost breaking. I had found my place right on the edge; I could look down and see everyone, and then I woke up.

Early the next morning on New Year's Day, I started out on my usual five mile run, reflecting on the previous night's dream.... knowing this day was the end of my isolation, for today was the wedding of my very close friends.

Shortly after starting my run, I met a friend who runs marathons and happened to be headed in the same direction. Running side-by-side for a couple miles proved a catalyst for reliving and re-experiencing my dream. Just as in the dream, a pervasive energy induced a feeling of being able to run forever. My thoughts and sad feelings relived the destruction of both the Christmas tree and my apartment. I just kept running and running; I felt like my emotions and the energy I had felt in the dream were now empowering me. While I ran, I was able to connect with a variety of people. I felt that I was emanating positive energy as I ran. I was smiling, and people were responding as if they knew me. With this connecting energy that beamed out of me, I ran by a whole bunch of gang members. My smile and energy captivated them so much they smiled back with a sincerity that touched me. Running down side streets and back alleys, I felt invincible.

Never having run over five or six miles, I had now run well over 17miles and was near my ex-wife's house. I stopped for a moment at a little metaphysical church for reflection, then went two doors down to see her. I told her what had been happening to me: about Judy, the dream, and now this experience of running 17miles. She hugged and comforted me. Later she gave me a ride back to my apartment in time to get ready for the wedding that afternoon.

After taking a shower, I was surprised that although my muscles were sore, I still had this energy going through me. I was awake…I was awake in a spectacular way. It was out of the ordinary – I felt alive in a new way.

At the wedding, I felt strong contradictory feelings. Seeing my friends so happy together brought up strong feelings of grief about Judy and me. The ceremony had been powerful and the music wonderfully touching. My whole being just opened up. Strangely enough, along with my grief, something was still moving through me, empowering me with a feeling of ecstasy. Even with my deep grief, I continued to ride this high feeling that had carried me all day.

At home, after the wedding, this powerful energy continued to run through me. I felt compelled to take a walk; it was like something was pulling me. After a 17-mile run and a wedding, I was awed by this force pulling me. It was the same energy that had pulled me on the run. I had no choice but to comply; I soon noticed I was following my feet, watching where they were going. I had the feeling I was an observer, separate from my body. I could see where my body was going, but I wasn't directing it. I yielded myself to this experience.

I was walking down the very beach I had ran down early that morning. I saw myself walking directly for the life guard station where Judy and I had spent so much time together, taking pictures and enjoying the beach. When I reached the lifeguard station, I saw on the other side three burnt Christmas trees. Tears again welled up in my eyes; I wanted to stop, but I couldn't. This energy would not let me. Literally following my feet down the beach over to Second Street in Belmont Shores I walked, passing many stores. My curiosity peaked as my feet took me into a record store.

I had no inclination of what I was doing there or what I was looking for; I was just being guided. Now without prompting, my hands reached into a section I would not ordinarily look in, classical music. Without reading labels, my hands selected several albums, and I bought them. I felt I was supposed to buy these albums, even though classical music was not what I was accustomed to buying. One album, "The Theme from Chariots of Fire," was from a movie that Judy and I had seen together.

I returned home and played "Chariots of Fire" with the speakers full blast. Without any alcohol or drugs, I was carried away into another dimension, the music resonating with the same ecstatic energy that had moved me all day. I felt

lifted up into a state of consciousness out of my ordinary experiences – like my whole life was being orchestrated
through me for my viewing. I was re-experiencing my entire
life – including childhood, kindergarten, parochial school, my
experience with Jesus, all my experiences in this world –
with key moments highlighted, like the day my grandmother
died. Out of the shadows, within a flash, came every face of
every person I had ever met. In this consciousness, I danced
around the world in ecstasy and grief.

The previous week had been filled with figuring out and
analyzing. Now my mind was totally exhausted, totally dead,
dropping away into something much bigger than my personal
self. I yielded to this greater state of knowing. My whole
world had died – I suddenly became aware of surrender as
the solution to my experiences; this was totally contrary to
the use of self-will and self-responsibility that I had been
pursuing for several years with existential thinking.

Now I had a new perspective, which was far more significant to me than anything. Judy became my angel on a
mission to reawaken my spiritual life by catapulting me into
the underworld of my unfinished past and one-sided life.
Although I had resolved that Judy was not to be the woman
of my life, she had completed her mission. I was now enriched with a part of myself I had long ago abandoned. I am
very grateful for this reawakening which, in looking back,
has dramatically changed my life over the last 14 years.

Sarah's Story

Hit On The Head

"I want to go back to America...I want to go back to America."

I was told I said these words many, many times while in a coma. I slightly remember it but only vaguely. People would come into my hospital room who acted like they knew me, but I didn't know them! Some spoke Japanese and I felt I should be able to understand, but I couldn't. It was awful. Most of the patients were elderly. Some acted strange. It was all so confusing. What was I doing in this cold hospital room filled with foreigners and unfamiliar faces?

With the help of my parents and friends, I began to paste my past back together. I remember going to Japan as a foreign exchange student. I wanted to experience another culture and educational system. Having high expectations of myself, I was pleased to participate and succeed in this exchange program.

As with most things that I set my mind to, I began to learn Japanese and settled into my unique environment. I soon gained an intimate understanding and living sense of the culture, since I was one of the few students who lived off-campus with a Japanese family. I was particularly fond of my Japanese surrogate mother. We liked each other and had many fun times together. I remember having both Japanese and American friends.

The week before my accident, I wrote my mother and questioned her about whether or not I was going to die young. I have always been intuitive, so maybe I was having a premonition. Soon, those cryptic words faded out of my awareness as I went about my daily activities. Then, on what seemed to be just another ordinary day, the events of my life took a sudden and dramatic change.

I was on my way to school, riding down a bike path which crossed a one-way street. I neither saw nor remembered what hit me. I was told, though, that a man had crashed into me so hard that I went flying head-first into a brick wall several feet away. The next thing I remembered was my dad pushing me in a wheelchair, two-and-a-half weeks after the accident.

Everything was blurry and out of focus, as Dad wheeled me around the hospital grounds. The first things I remember were being outside and seeing the wind-blown trees. It was like I was in a fishbowl; I guess my brain was still recovering. Fortunately, I did remember who my parents were, but I couldn't speak or remember a word of Japanese, and I no longer remembered any of my fellow students who visited me in the hospital.

My mother said they received the news via an answering machine message. The disembodied voice explicitly told about the severity of my accident and the likelihood of my death, advising my parents to remain at home. When my mother told me, I was shocked! I can't imagine how they felt. Now I was glad to be alive, to be given a second chance, and I so wanted to make the most of it.

Within two months, I was back home in America, living with my parents, but I soon realized my life was not the same. I was 20 pounds underweight, which was a lot for my body frame. I would eat like a horse without gaining a pound, which worried everyone. Several times a week, my parents would take me to UCLA for neurological exams. With wires attached to my head and graphs running all the time, I looked and felt like a monster. Besides, I was used to being independent, and now I felt like a caged animal, a scientifically scrutinized rat. Along with all the medical treatments, my parents nervously watched over me, making me feel like I was back in junior high. "Leave me the fuck alone!" I remember cursing at my parents, which was totally out of character. I had these mood swings which seemed to be exacerbated when my decisions were questioned, challenging my adulthood.

Several weeks passed, and although I still had headaches, my body was physically back to normal, and I was a little bit more civil. Still, I was tired of the medical tests and the overprotection of my parents; I wanted to get back in the swing of things, and classes at the university started in a month. I had a lot of dreams and goals I wanted to fulfill. At the university, there were some graduate courses and an internship that I was very interested in taking. Now I was determined to get back into the flow; I had always been a high achiever with high expectations of myself.

I returned to Berkeley, taking a full load and one graduate course, with the pride and confidence associated with high grades and academic success. But things did not work out like I had planned; I was failing all my subjects. I would read and study, but I couldn't perform like before. I became very terrified and imagined all these worst-case scenarios. Could I even graduate from college? Would I end up in some menial job like selling hamburgers on a street corner? My mind was slanting everything to the negative.

I began sleeping more while staying in bed longer. I would mope around the dorm, feeling like nothing was every going to turn out right. Things that used to please me, like sunsets and flowers, seemed unimportant. My boyfriend of over a year left me, which made things worse. He couldn't deal with my changes. This was a real blow. I thought for sure that he above all others would stand by me. As my emotions tumbled down, I began thinking more and more about my bleak future, and being perfectionistic by nature, dramatized everything.

The vibrant me disappeared, bringing a sense of confusion to my friends and family. I felt trapped; I knew who I used to be, but I couldn't reach it. It was like being in a cage, knowing that you had a key, but not remembering how to get out. I felt paralyzed. This was not the body I remembered. I wanted my body, my life back!

As Christmas time rolled around, I was looking forward to returning to my family, because things couldn't get much worse. Unknowingly I needed my family's support, but when I got home I learned that Mom and Dad had decided to take their vacation before Christmas. This meant I was home alone much of the time, since my sisters were already living on their own. All day long I thought about having a second chance to live, but with no idea of how to use it. This really bothered me, especially since everything was going so badly. How was I going to make it in life when I didn't feel like I fit in my own body?

I started contemplating ending it all. I was confused. I had lost whatever it was that was me, and I didn't feel like I had a future. What did I have to live for? A few nights before Christmas, I went down to my parents' bathroom and stared into the medicine cabinet. My mother was a nurse, so there were plenty of pills. I started pouring them into my hand. I thought about how much and which ones I would have to take to kill myself. If I was going to do it, I wanted to make sure I took enough; it was going to be all or nothing. I wasn't about to end up a zombie.

Bending over with my hands wrapped around my waist, I felt tears streaming down my red cheeks. What was I doing?

Why was my life going so badly? Why did my boyfriend leave me? I missed him so much; I was lonely. I cried for a long, long time. I had lost so much; I was no fun to be around any more, and my friends were starting to shy away. Who could I count on? Who was going to be there for me? I cried until the tears stopped flowing.

All of a sudden I was a floating essence, and in a snap I was looking down and viewing my own body. Everything disappeared except this aerial view of myself. I wasn't aware of what was floating, just that I was looking down at me.

At first, everything seemed cloudy and dreary, as though I were looking through fog. Then as I looked down at myself, I saw a dramatic change, a transformation from dark to light, which shifted how I saw and perceived who I was.

A voice from within me said, "Look at what you are doing!" This statement reverberated through my consciousness – it was deeper than just the thoughts and actions related to suicide. It was the fact that I had been dying all along – depressed and self-tortured by wanting to be who I had been, instead of who and what I was now.

The voice sang through my body with a kind of pep talk. The cajoling message comforted me with this declaration: everything would be fine if I would just allow myself to move through this difficult part of my life. It assured me that my life was worth living, with many things up ahead. This incredible feeling/thought reached down to the core of my being with the belief that I would be a stronger person for having persevered through this painful time. It was this experience, this belief, that saved my life.

As quickly as I had become the floating form, I was back in my body, but my life's perspective had been transformed with a new conscious awareness. Back in the bathroom and in my body, I slowly put all the pills back into their bottles. Then I walked out into the backyard which looks over a lake. The lake's rippling water, and the star-filled night, all coalesced into a calming ambiance. Now, whether life's changes are good or bad – I remind myself: I'm alive; if I fall down and I can get back up again. I believe in myself.

Ostad Hadi Parvarandeh

Attention to God

I was born in Tehran on May 12, 1926. As a boy, I remember my father was a very spiritual man which influenced me because I was always thinking about God and spiritually related subjects: What is God? What is death? Why do people have cancer? I yearned to help cure people of cancer. Seeking a cool breeze after hot days in Tehran, I often slept on the roof. Before falling asleep, I would gaze at the stars and the vast sky with awe and wonder. As I looked up into the heavens, I could feel an energy force throughout my entire body. I often had out-of-body experiences, voyaging into space.

When I was in my early teens, I noticed I had a curious affect on my sister. Once in a while, during casual conversations her eyes would suddenly close; at first I thought that she had simply fallen asleep. I would shake her and would say, " Okay, get up." She would wake up and wonder what had happened to her. After this occurred several times, I made an investigation into what was happening to her. I found out that somehow she was being hypnotized. I began exploring and reading about this subject, while hypnotizing her on a regular basis. I soon discovered that she could have out of body experiences as I'd had as a boy using hypnotic trance.

With hypnosis, I was able to send her to many places in the world gathering astoundingly accurate details and information. Once my brother-in-law was lost during the Second World War after joining the Russian partisan. Using my sister as a medium, I hypnotized her and asked if she could find him. "I can," she said immediately. She went on to say specifically where he could be located, in what city, house, and the exact room. No one could believe it, so we made a trip to the city. It was late at night when we arrived. I knocked on the door of the house and our brother-in-law answered and was greatly astonished to see us.

I had many kinds of these experiences with my sister, but what I dreamed of was finding a cure for cancer. While experimenting with hypnosis on my sister, I asked her if she could have contact with Hippocrates, the famous Greek physician. Surprisingly, while under hypnosis she began talking with him. She again was my medium. I asked her to question him about the treatment and remedies for cancer. Although he and I had a dialog through my sister, the answer that came back was "I don't know." I was very disappointed with the answers I received about the treatment of diseases, and so I began trying hypnosis as a healing agent. Still in the back of my youthful mind was the idea to help cure cancer and other physical aliments.

Throughout my youth and adolescence, I continued to focus my attention on God. Through my prayers and observations I began to realize that we are all in a symbolic way representations of the Divine. This made me feel very connected to everything: plants, animals, objects and especially human beings. I began to recognize that there was a collective force that ran through everything and everyone. This divine energy has some sort of collective consciousness that exists throughout the universe. As I attuned deeply through prayer to God I was increasingly able to feel this energy within myself, although I still had no way of knowing its full power or potential. All I knew was I had a deep respect for all of life and all the things in life. I deepened with this respect and love, noticing all the time this energy in my body.

A short time later a neighbor asked me to accompany her to visit a friend in the hospital. I went with her out of courtesy, feeling that she felt unsafe going alone. I was surprised when she asked me a second and then a third time to accompany her to the hospital. I said no. I didn't know the patient or her family and could see no reason to keep visiting someone I didn't know, but my neighbor told me that her friend had requested that I come because she always felt better. Slowly I began to speculate that maybe the energies in my body I had felt throughout my youth and adolescence were somehow affecting this lady positively. Shortly after my experience with my neighbor's friend, my grandmother told me she was suffering continual facial pain. I concentrated on her pain. When I touched her face with my hands, her pain was lifted suddenly for the first time in years. I began utilizing this energy with friends and relatives with their pain being diminished or eliminated.

Gradually, while in high school, I began to realize and examine the potential of this energy as people came to my home for healing. I could see that the individuals coming to me were feeling better or were cured completely. Once I was visiting the famous mosque, Chahar Bagh in the city of Esfahan. As I walked past one of the students, I sensed that he was feeling some pain. "Do you have pain?" I asked. The student's eyes opened wide and with an amazed look on his face – he said, "yes." I asked him where the pain was and he said in his feet. I bent down touching his feet while concentrating on the Divine, and the pain was lifted. This experience, taught me I could also diagnose the health of an individual. One day my cousin phoned me complaining of a migraine headache. I visualized him and the pain he was suffering; the pain stopped. I knew then there were no physical boundaries to this gift of healing. Neither distance nor place was a factor with this energy.

I didn't want to make money and my livelihood from healing other people. I felt that this gift was Divine in nature and should be given free, as a gentle breeze of fresh air or the numinous feeling created by a star-filled night is bestowed free to all. Therefore, I continued my education and upon graduation worked in the Ministry of Education in Tehran. I've worked as the General Director of the Culture and Fine Arts Division and was a Cultural Counselor for the countries of Greece, Turkey, and Yugoslavia. After retirement I devoted most of my time to healing and sharing this blessed gift of the Almighty.

As with everything a person attends to, I have grown in awareness and skill over the years. With every experience of different diseases and their sources, I have become intuitively better able to know and heal. For instance, if someone has a lung disease, I will quickly understand it and its causes. Sometimes conventional medicine has no diagnosis for a particular individual; but often, I am aware of the specific aliment that person is suffering in less than a minute.

I can be aware of specific diseases and aliments because the universe has a collective consciousness that connects everything and everyone. All information about diseases or anything else is instantaneously known throughout the universe. All of my life I have attended to the enormous vastness of the Almighty. I have become on open receptacle to this collective information which is known at the level of every atom. For instance, when I ask about a person's particular aliment, the collective consciousness informs me instantaneously with the answer.

I am a conduit through which the Divine energy of the universe flows. This Divine energy is what creates healing in those who come to see me. This energy is intelligent. It automatically goes to the area of the body that requires healing. All I need to do is be passively open to its movement. The physical sensations that are felt by the individual may range from vibrations to warmth or even cold. Since the energy in the universe is infinite, I feel no sense of loss with the transfer of energy.

In Tehran I have taught the power of healing to others. Today, there are twelve doctors and eight non-professional staff that apply healing energy to various patients. The Institute where patients are seen doesn't charge and welcomes all without regard to religion, race, wealth or a person's ethics. I believe that this Divine Energy is for everyone. God is the source of my gift, and I believe it belongs to anyone that needs it.

Students who come to learn the gift of healing usually train by my side for many months. Those that have a gift for healing are easy to discern. Those are people who have a deep drive or urge to serve or benefit mankind. Their purity of purpose is reflected in the effect they have on the person they are healing. It is quite simple: if the effect is positive then the student is moving with the right attention.

Some have asked why can I heal with Divine Energy while others are ineffective? The process of healing is not completely known even by myself. Someone who wants to learn how to play the piano must practice and dedicate his life to be able to perform well and with the grace of God that person may even become a master pianist.

My life is a reflection of what I have done with great dedication and focus, and that is to attend to the Divine Energy of the universe. Being open to the Almighty is my passion.

Thea Robertshaw

Another life: This Troubled Day Wasn't All There Was

At the age of 40 my life was both painful and stressful. My second child had just been born, and I was working full time at Brooks College. My 6½ year old adopted son came to us emotionally wounded from the foster care system. He was now 13 and hanging around with the wrong crowd and taking drugs. He made implied threats against the baby, and his many unsavory friends were intimidating the whole family. Often he would be out at all hours of the night causing me many restless nights worrying about him. It was hell, worse than the war years in Holland where I grew up.

I had recently graduated from California State University of Long Beach with a masters in drawing and painting. Although I had learned many fine artistic techniques, I was running out of inspirational ideas for future projects. I was daunted by my family chaos, my long hours at the college, and my lack of creative art projects when a friend invited me to join a dream group. I became thoroughly fascinated with our assigned book *Creative Dreaming* by Patricia Garfield, especially the chapter of the Senoi aboriginal people who used dreams in their daily lives. I began writing five dreams a night, sometimes more. All this dream work reminded me of the time I spent with my father when I was 16 years old.

Shortly after World War II, I remember sharing my dreams with my father, who was dying of lung cancer. We would come together for tea in the morning and share verbally our nightly adventures. Although this process was informal, I remember those last few years of his life as a very special time. Now I was keeping an accurate written journal of all my remembered dreams.

With my full and stressful life, it was a small miracle that I put so much time into dreams. I soon realized that my dreams were colorful and interesting. This inspired me to paint one. The first painting I did of a dream was both magical and mystical. While I was painting the dream I realized *my troubled day wasn't all there was.* I had another life, a psychic life, with all its feelings and experiences.

The first dream I painted went as follows: I am on an ice landscape and I hear footsteps, the sound of boots coming towards me. As it gets louder, I suddenly see a golden figure appear. He has huge wings and golden fur, and I felt a beautiful, incredible feeling of connection; at times I feel like I merge with him. I walk under his wing with three unfamiliar children towards a twin engine airplane in the near distance, and as we move closer, the plane's wings really catch my attention.

In the silence of the late night with everyone in bed, I painted this numinous being with awe. As I manifested this winged figure a feeling of warmth permeated throughout my body. Now, I was deeply in touch with my inner life, drawing strength for daily coping and providing magical inspiration. Enriched and enlivened, I painted two more dreams with similar motifs.

After painting these dreams, I realized that my memories originated in the same inner landscape with similar qualities to my dreams. I decided to paint a war scene memory in honor of my father, who was my rock of Gibraltar with his support and strength. I remember being on the back of his bicycle passing a row of birch trees which my father always said would light the way no matter how dark it was. Next, I saw some Germans shooting their cannons; then, I looked up, and a plane came down directly over our heads blazing on fire. As I painted this memory, I recalled feeling safe riding behind my father through this horrifying experience. Painting this experience deepened and expanded my understanding of my inner world, teaching me that memories, images, and symbols lived on within me regardless of what was happening in my outer life.

After painting the war scene memory, I went back to painting my dreams. I painted a prophetic dream about my 80-year-old aunt who lived with us. Again, this dream took place in a far North-wintry scene with snow-capped mountains in the background. My aunt wearing a fur coat is walking away while my niece is riding in a horse and carriage passing by. I painted this scene depicting my aunt walking away in three different places on a large 4 X 5 foot high canvas. Looking directly at me in the foreground of this dark cold setting is a black dog with blue feathers around its neck. It was another numinous mythological creature that inhabited many of my dreams. This dream foreshadowed my aunt's death and my eventual life transformation through the medium of dreams.

As my interest in mythology, Jungian psychology, and my inner dreams grew, I experienced a prophetic dream about the difficulties my second son and I faced. He was following in my adoptive son's footsteps and creating another family crisis. This dream illustrated what Jung meant when he said, "where you live – its indigenous people's mythology will get under your skin." Although the locale of the major dream image wasn't exact, Jung's point was exemplified by the following dream which took me many years to fully understand:

In this dream, my twelve year old son and I are walking past a forest with his dog Trieste at our side. I noticed that facing the forest was a row of theater seats and next to them was a snake with a red feather – the color red really attracted my attention. In the dream's next scene, I have a thought that the dog should kill the snake – that's her job. Immediately, I think the dog might get hurt which would upset my son very much. Regardless, I know that I can't take the thought back and it's going to happen. I'm very stressed out as the dog and snake face each other in attack mode. I try to protect my son as the dog grabs the snake by the head, and I feel a sense of fright run throughout my body knowing that to kill the snake, the dog must seize it by the neck. I'm in an emotional daze when suddenly the snake transforms into a child with pieces falling off its face like the shedding of skin – the child looks Oriental but not exactly.

All that day the dreamed filled me with a buzzing energy. It became such a living part of my daily activities that I had to share it with someone in the hope of stabilizing its ever present energy. I chose one of my older students who was very knowledgeable about Aztec mythology. She said, "Thea you've dreamed about the plumed serpent, Quetzalcoatl." I then remembered that the Aztecs and Mayans sometimes had Oriental features, especially their eyes and noses.

This was probably the most incredible dream of my life. I painted it in three distinct scenes called a triptych, the style of many old religious paintings reflecting their spiritual importance. The most exciting, numinous, and transformational point in the dream was when the snake changed into a boy with shedding skin. This was very difficult to paint because I wanted to get some transparency between them, illustrating and highlighting this important symbol of transition. Certainly, the dream predicted a lot of trouble, pain and eventual transformation for both my son and me.

Jung said that when we have a big dream we need to do something with it, or it will just fade back into the unconscious where it came from. As I worked on this project, several interesting coincidences occurred which Jung calls synchronicity. For instance, Jack Valonski televised a 60 minute documentary on the Aztec myth of Quetzalcoatl, the chief God in their religion. In the myth, his heart was ripped from his chest to become a star in the heavens. My son watched this show with me and said, "Mother, get rid of the painting." A few days later, my son came to me with a snake dream of his own. He'd dreamt of the concrete circle at the side of our house which had plants all around it. In the dream my son is face to face with an anaconda. At this precarious eye to eye confrontation the dream ends. As my son's counterpart to my dream indicated, we definitely were in for some frightening times ahead.

Another fascinating element to this painting was that I painted a dark figure that wasn't even in the dream. I don't know why I painted it behind my son and me, but when the dark figure appeared, I didn't want to get rid of it.

The artistic process reveals and transforms with serendipity, the adding and subtracting of elements through the creative process. Dreams, symbols, and images can also have this unpredictable and timeless multi-layered quality. When we remember our dreams and manifest them in an external medium like painting, they can enhance, change, and deepen us with their symbolic wisdom. We don't always need to know a dream's exact message. Sometimes, they simply give us a feeling and sense of hope knowing that they come from a deep spiritual connection within us.

My father had reared me in a fundamentalist Christian sect. Although he was somewhat fanatical, there was a certain beauty to the depth of his faith which I respected very highly. For instance, during the war he chose to hide Jews even though this brought great risk to all our lives – this is really living your faith. Unfortunately, this kind of Christian religion really puts the fear in you and over time I lost my belief in religion and spirituality. Later, I read the *Age of Reason* by Thomas Payne which really shattered my childlike naiveté. As I look back on that part of my life, I realize I developed a conviction that religion and spirituality were mostly misinterpreted, and I was determined not to allow it to influence my life anymore.

As I continued to explore my inner landscape with dream mythologies, symbols, and images, my beliefs and ideas about spirituality and life began to change. I remembered that there was a somewhat covert tradition of healers and psychics in my family. My father had told me several stories about my paternal grandmother's healing abilities. He said, as a young boy, his family immigrated to a small village in Germany where many of the villagers would come to her for treatment of physical, mental, or traumatic injuries. She never talked about it; she was probably afraid of repercussions from the dominant Christian religion. Although she never taught her children, my uncle learned to be a hands-on healer. He let me feel the electromagnetic energy pulsate through his hands, showing me how it worked and telling me how he discovered it.

After the big Quetzalcoatl dream, I felt at a loss, threatened, and despondent about the situation with my son. I had been thinking about a pilgrimage to a holy place and decided to walk with my son the six days on the Inca road to visit Machu Picchu in Peru. I started breaking in the special hiking boots that I had purchased for the trip, but just prior to our departure, I developed a sore spot on my foot. Because of the intense pain, I realized I had no choice but to abandon the trip. Several days later, I received a flyer announcing a five day workshop with Michael Harner, a shaman. The workshop's shamanic material was closely connected to my dream work and initiated me into a deeper understanding of the unconscious and the art of healing – culminating in a profound adventurous experience.

On the fourth day of our work, Michael Harner said that he wanted to demonstrate the Northwest Coast Indians' canoe communal healing journey. He wanted someone from our diverse group of 40 (including doctors, nurses, therapist, a priest and a minister) to ask for a healing. I had this incredible debate within myself about asking for a healing. Who am I to ask for a healing? I don't have cancer or any major trauma. Nonetheless, I had this strong sense that I had to ask for a healing. So I did.

When I met with him, Harner asked me why I thought I needed a healing. I told him that I believe my son was in danger, and how this had sapped my energy making me feel very weak. I couldn't verbalize much more than these few comments.

Later, when we came together again, Michael said, " I have chosen Thea for healing." Then he instructed us on how to form the shape of a canoe using everyone in the group, and at that point I was placed on the medicine rug and told to stay present in my everyday reality. He told everyone to sound out their power animal while he went on his healing journey. Three drums began to beat signaling the start. The drum's heartbeat rhythm takes the shaman into other realms. The animal sounds evoked a feeling of being in a jungle. It was a strange experience being present while others were going into altered states. I watched Michael as he sang his power song and used his rattle; I heard his voice distinctly change as he journeyed into the sacred dimension. He lay down next to me on the medicine rug journeying into deeper realms via the sound of the drums, returning with my power animal. He blew the animal's power into my heart and head, telling me that at this time my healing power would be the greatest. He said I would have to dance my power animal, and if I felt moved to touch someone – I was to do so.

At that moment I felt on-the-spot because dancing in front of 40 people was not my thing, but I said to myself drop it – you just have to do this. So as I danced my power animal, I felt like I had to touch this priest from Canada. For some reason this man was aversive to me. I would have walked around the block to avoid him, but by reassuring myself with supportive self-talk, I was able to let go of these feelings, went over, and lovingly touched him. As I continued my dance near the front of the canoe, there was a woman who had kept pretty much to herself. Although I had little contact with her during the workshop, I felt I had to touch her. The moment I did, a flood of tears came out that lasted for hours – it took five people to tend to her.

When I was moved to stop my animal dance, I went over and stood by Michael. He said to everyone, "You see this is how it works! Thea didn't know, but the two people she touched had also asked me for a healing."

At that moment my rational mind was mystified, but somehow during the dance of my power animal I knew. This experience validated my own intuition and my own spiritual connection to the Other. I received a healing that day, but more importantly I was initiated into a greater way of knowing. I learned to trust it – to trust this spiritual connection. When I was dancing I knew the Other at some level and That will always be with me. I didn't receive a vision; the heavens didn't open; God didn't speak to me, but my journey on the path and way of the Other began.

The way towards the Other takes time – one needs to deepen in trust.

About six years after my initial dream painting, while I continued pursuing shamanic teachings and the art of healing, I had a dream that taught me even more about the relationship between the external and inner life. Because I had actively continued my dream work, I quickly realized that it was a recurring dream. The unconscious signifies its importance through repetition. I needed to pay attention to this dream:

I'm in the middle of a makeshift bridge without any handrails. The whining noise of engines from an airplane bomber grows louder and louder. I feel trapped and terrified; soon the vibrating moan is completely surrounding me – **I can't get away.** My hands instinctively cover my ears. The noise becomes unbearable; I wake up in a state of fright.

During the war years in Holland, they built wooden walkways across the canals after the bridges were bombed and destroyed. As a little girl, it was very frightening to cross them because the water was so cold. To swim in that frigid water was unthinkable; to fall in meant almost certain death.

Although war scenes are not aesthetically pleasing to me, I knew I needed to paint this dream. Painting this sound dream was difficult because I needed to find a way to visually picture the fright created by the sound. So, I painted the little girl screaming while holding her hands over her ears, and in the background were sound waves coming from a World War II bomber. In order to make it realistic I researched WWII bombers and spent much time choosing the right colors that portrayed the feelings I'd experienced in the dream. According to Jung, we can't always express the feelings and thoughts related to images because they are pre-language. Thus other mediums like painting, dancing, poetry, theater, and film allow for these images to be expressed more fully. *The greatest thing about painting this dream was that it never came back!*

I realized that we can affect our unconscious by what we do in the everyday world and that the unconscious can affect us as was illustrated in my healing experience with Michael Harner. This painting really encouraged me to work with others on their inner landscapes. Later, I began shamanic inner journeying via drumming to discover others' power animals and help in their healing. To journey back and forth between the unconscious and conscious worlds is a wonderful experience. As an artist it allows me a rich landscape of images from which to create my paintings. As a shamanic healer, it helps me empower others with healing and inspiration.

My dreams have given me a great gift, for which I'm very grateful.

Ken's Story

After spending a month in the hospital for colitis, I was totally outraged when I walked into the new store. What the hell had they done to my plans. I was the one in charge of the store's layout and design – who screwed them up? I confronted the manager, "Are you crazy! What the hell did you do to my plans?"

"Look, Ken, in your absence we made a few changes." I went ballistic. "who the hell gives you the right to make changes?"

"Now calm down, Ken; you don't have to get all bent out of shape." I lost it and hit him right across the face. I told him to leave things the way they're supposed to be. Fortunately, it was just a glancing blow, and in hindsight, I know I was still a little emotionally unstable from the colitis and my hospital stay. Nonetheless, I was pissed-off; they had totally destroyed all of the work and effort I had done for the grand opening.

In the early Sixties, my life was this crazy all the time. I was under a great deal of stress and pressure from my client, the Riviera Sofa Bed Company. I was an interior designer in charge of preparing new stores for their grand openings. Throughout the company the tension was enormous – the company was in an expansion phase, opening new stores throughout California. I was extremely nervous and high strung by nature which, combined with the job pressures, exacerbated my colitis.

At that time, I was under the care of a doctor and taking cortisone four times a day. I had built up spurs on my foot from the cortisone which made the use of my right leg pain-

ful. Having difficulty walking made me realize the value of
exploring alternative approaches. I was introduced to nutri-
tional supplements which seemed to help because I began to
feel much better. Someone suggested that I go on a fast to
clear out all the toxins from the medication. It sounded like a
good idea, so I did.

Without any supervision, I went on a bananas and water
fast. With my particular type of bleeding colitis, I was losing
about a cup of blood a day which my body was struggling to
replace. The strain of the fast combined with the blood loss
made me very weak. One morning I went into shock. Somehow, I managed to crawl to the front door of my apartment,
but I could move no farther – I felt helpless and vulnerable. I
knew I was dying – I closed my eyes.

Moments later a white light appeared. It was brighter
than a flood light but not invasive or threatening. I knew I
was dying, but still I felt a sense of awe and peace. Elation
ran through my body with a release of energy like when
you're pushing your hand hard against something and you
pull it back. My negative beliefs and feelings took on a different perspective. Thoughts like: things aren't going to
work, and life is crummy were being transformed. I realized I
didn't have to think like that way anymore. It was an a-ha
experience. If I turned around from the negative, my life
would be much better. It was so obvious; I don't have to
walk into a fire, I can walk away from it. As simple as this
seems, it was a complete shift in my high strung way of life
and awareness.

My communication with this light was more of a feeling
than direct answers. I remember feeling how messed-up my
life was; how I had made so many mistakes. I knew I deserved to die, but I pleaded for a chance to make it better. In
a non-verbal and non-thought way, I got answers to many

questions. It was more of a knowing and feeling than an intellectual, logical answer. As the light disappeared, everything seemed to be okay. I was able to drag myself over to the phone and called a friend. It seemed like only seconds before I was whisked off to the hospital in an ambulance.

The news was not good. The doctor told me that without treatment I would have been dead in a couple of hours, then things proceeded to get worst. The next morning an intern mistakenly took away my glucose intravenous treatment, and I became delusional with bizarre behavior, really quite insane. I was taken to the psychiatric ward where my arms and legs were put into restraints. Somehow, I squirmed and wriggled my hands free and I began gnawing on my own hand. I still have the scar where I had eaten out my own flesh.

Later that same day, they gave me a blood transfusion that was about 65 degrees, way below normal body temperature. It felt like a pint of ice shooting through my veins. My body began freezing, and I went into shock again. I was right on the edge of death when something in my mind said, don't go. Stay. You have a purpose. You are to help others.

The doctors later told me that my fast caused a depletion of potassium in my body resulting in a form of insanity. Fortunately, two doctors, a father and son, from the Philippines were on my ward. They provided me with the proper medicine and nutrients to fully recover – Two months later I was back to work.

What a wild ride! In such a relatively short period of time, I went from being close to death to literally being insane. But the peace and awe of the white light experience had transformed my perception and had made my experiences bearable.

Things were different when I returned to work; I was far less negative and more at peace. I realized through the dialog with the white light that I needed to take responsibility to change my life's attitudes and behaviors. With the white light's peaceful feeling as my guide, I have focused on my purpose through all of life's ups and downs. Not to long after returning home from the hospital, I began to work with teenagers. My goal was to excite them with life's possibilities, hoping to help steer them away from drugs and negativity. Although I was unpaid, I've found the rewards of helping others rich and abundant.

Even after the experience with the white light, my life has had its struggles. For example, not long after my near-death experience, I rented a house so I could start an in home business. I was confident that I would be successful in this new venture. The night after Christmas a fire broke out. I remember the flames shooting up all around me – I barely made it out alive. Watching my memories, possessions and dreams go up in smoke was very painful. I felt overwhelmed, and became depressed.

Survival was very tenuous for a long time after the fire, I was forced to live as a nomad, changing housing accommodations frequently. Still, I had this inner feeling, an inner knowing – things were going to work out okay no matter how many obstacles that I had to endure and overcome. I certainly was depressed and in grief over my losses with the fire. However, recalling the peaceful feeling engendered by my white light experience, I know it's my responsibility to handle all of what life serves up with my primary focus being the effort to change my attitude and behavior. Now, I am much more able to yield to what life has to offer, using my capabilities to their fullest, knowing that peace is always available no matter what my circumstance.

I am worthy and can contribute to life. I am grateful for what feels like a second chance. A chance to embrace life with the peace of my white light experience.

Vicki Walker's Story

My Sister Talked Me into Taking the Class

I told my sister, "Oh yeah, sure, sure, maybe I'll take the classes when I can find someone to ride with every week from Los Angeles to San Diego." I didn't mean it; I was just talking. There was no way I saw myself taking a class every week in San Diego when I lived in Downey. I occasionally visited my sister and even went to a couple of the group's parties, but driving over 200 miles every week was out of the question!

Sunday, several weeks later, when I was visiting with my sister, she said, "Classes are starting in two weeks and there is a family driving down from Arcadia who can give you a ride."

I said, "Okay, okay, then I'll go." I thought to myself that traveling once a week for three months to take classes in San Diego seemed absurd. So much for rational thinking – I began the classes.

It was in my third class that Ann Meyer – who is one of the founders of Teaching of the Inner Christ – and her two meditation assistants began setting up for the meditations. In the first two meditations, we closed our eyes and went into a very deep and relaxed state. I felt and heard the deep rhythmic pounding of my heart beating. It was quite intense but nothing too out of the ordinary. In the third meditation we were all in a circle, and Ann was standing behind me, feeding power and energy with her open hands held towards me and the rest of group. The ambiance of loving energy was profound. I felt a surge of spiritual energy throughout my body, and I was literally compelled to stand right up out of my chair – I just had to stand; the energy was that strong!

Everyone in the class seemed moved by this particular meditation.

After the surge of energy, I went back into a relaxed peaceful state. As the energy permeated my body, I felt a metamorphosis taking place within me. It was like coming home again to a place I had somehow lost. It was a wonderful state of being. Later, Ann said that connecting to the Inner Christ would come easier for me because I had probably already made my Inner Christ contact earlier in my life. This peaceful inner space is what I now call my God-conscious awareness, or Christ Self, as it is called in the teachings.

Although we are moved by many small experiences in life such as when touched by a significant dream or a momentary "Aha" experience, they often are fleeting and have little staying power. In this meditation something dramatic happened that changed my conscious awareness. Suddenly, I was connected to an unbelievable power that filled me with spiritual illumination. It was comparable to being Born Again in the Christian tradition. I went from being attached to the outer world to being aware of an infinite connection, a higher source, sense, and power that was within me. Now, I could go inside and feel that powerful sense of love, comfort and ability which had been there all along.

Later I learned that this surge of energy was called a power feeding. This is where spiritual energy comes into the physical body and mind of an individual. Through this energy force, a metaphorical lifting and distilling of the body and mind functions are augmented with a sense of well-being and great joy. With a great power feeding the body may shake or quiver and usually signals a progression in spiritual development and awareness. I have had many such power feedings since that initial meditation.

One such experience lasted for two weeks; I felt disoriented and not my usual self, as if I were observing myself from the outside as others might see me. When I returned to San Diego for another deep meditation, I received tremendous energy that went throughout my body. I perspired heavily as I became rather hot. Words began coming into my mind telling me about the prior two weeks of intense energy. It revealed that the powerful energy called C.A.I.M or Christ Awareness in Man had been pouring into my body; and sometimes our bodies may resist spiritual energy and change. As I received this information, I felt a shift to a greater level of knowing or awareness. Immediately, my disorientation dissipated and I felt at ease and serene. Old beliefs and thoughts have continued to slowly be transformed and lifted out of me to this present day.

Before my initial breakthrough meditation and the beginning of my studies, I was certainly in need of a great change. I had many behaviors and attitudes that were both unhealthy and destructive. I was taking a variety of illegal drugs, even growing marijuana in my backyard. I was dating several men and was quite confused and unsettled. Nonetheless, slowly and over time my perspective and approach to life began transforming, and I started developing a new awareness about what was healthy and best for me. As they were offered, I began taking classes, one after another. With each class a growing new perspective and truth was revealed, bringing me joy, surprise, and excitement. After many classes and much study, I began teaching courses in Southern California which helped me develop a greater sense of responsibility. I used the discipline I learned through teaching by going back to school to earn my masters degree in counseling.

Through the years, my awareness and connection to my higher spiritual source has grown; however, I soon learned this didn't mean that everything in life was going to be smooth and easy. After starting a center in Long Beach, I remember feeling incredibly sad driving home from work one day – I don't even remember why. My gloomy mood was accompanied by thoughts of how easy it would be to let go of everything and leave it all behind, starting my life over in some new place. As I drove close to the coast, I took the beach drive and soon pulled the car over to park. I got out and began walking on the grass along the shore. All the time my mind was on a fast treadmill: I'll just leave, no one will know. I'll move to another place. I'll start over. Nobody will ever know where I am. All of a sudden I heard this little voice within me say, "Just turn around." I stopped in my tracks and turned around and started walking in the opposite direction. In an instant I completely knew that to change my thinking was to change my experience. In a snap my thinking changed and I was able to take in the beauty of the scene before me, the waves booming onto the shore, the blue sky, and the glorious sun. This simple truth has been a great gift and has made a great difference in my life. Now, I know my thoughts and emotions are much more fluid and that I can consciously shift them to meet the challenges I face in a more peaceful way.

Still, peace is not always with me. Apparently, to be carried away by my thoughts and feelings is inherent to my nature which sometimes overshadows my new learning and perspective. I remember driving on the freeway in a new Corolla, when without warning, the traffic stopped, and I crashed into the car ahead of me. Intense emotions flooded over me and I began to cry. In a few seconds my feelings changed into anger and I commenced yelling at the top of my lungs, "Okay God, I want to see the good out of this!" Just a few cars ahead of us was a policeman giving a citation; he called a tow truck which quickly arrived and removed my car and me from the anxiety and stress of the accident scene. I was towed to a garage where by chance an adjuster was already present from my insurance company which made my claim that much easier. The garage shop owner, a very nice man, gave me a ride to work 15 miles away. Now, without transportation back and forth to work, I decided to join a carpool because the repairs to my car were going to take some time.

Carpooling was a great adventure with lots of friendly people and interesting conversations. A buyer whom I talked with on a number of occasions was looking for an assistant and offered me a better paying job, which more than paid for my additional expenses due to the accident. When I originally made that challenge to God, I doubted any value could arise from the accident. Now I know that throughout all of life run infinite connections, and my awareness of these divine connections is more important than the outcomes they produce. They are the little lessons that remind me not to prejudge events and people because the human capacity to know is infinitesimally small compared to the great divine mystery. Besides, it is our faith in our conscious connection to the divine that engenders a sense of peace, serenity, and hope in our lives.

My growing awareness of the connection behind what seems to be everyday reality was initiated in that powerful meditation with Ann. Since then, I have seen more of the interdependent relationships between events. For example, six friends and I were all attending the International New Thought Alliance Conference. After the conclusion of the keynote address by Jack Bolen, we asked him if he would like to join us for dinner. He said yes, so we all went up to the rotating restaurant at the top of the hotel. Jack, a Unity minister, had a presence that felt like an eight foot circle of spiritual energy, which made him quite charismatic and powerful. By our determined effort, we sat next to the window with Jack in the middle and the rest of us along each side; the image and allusion of the last supper came to my mind as a metaphor for the scene. As Jack talked, the restaurant rotated to a point where the sun was directly behind me. Jack said to everyone, "Look at the sun behind her." With the radiant sunlight streaming in around me I felt this rush of energy throughout my body. Jack, with a sublime voice and expression, then said, "What do you want from your life?" His question was like an arrow shot straight for my heart, and when it hit the mark I was touched at the core of my being. My aura of sunlight and the depth of the question created an ambiance that awed and overwhelmed everyone. As if each were similarly struck by their own arrow, we all began to cry in unison. Somehow we were all spiritually connected in an experience that to this day continues to move me.

The question, "What do you want with your life," is something that everyone should ask themselves. I reflected on it for the next several days. I was determined to live this question in a more conscious manner. A week later, I prepared an affirmation chart describing what I want to bring into my life. The chart was divided into four sections. In the area for love relationship, I wrote a man like Jack Bolen or better. This was the kind of man I wanted in my life, and I was going to consciously confirm this affirmation.

Sometime later, I was given a gift of Jack's series of tapes called The Twelve Steps of Spiritual Awareness. My friend who had the first tape in the series lent it to his friend – Jim Walker really liked the tape and asked where he could get the rest of the them.

My friend said, "Well I really don't know for sure Jim but you might ask Vicki Harris."

When he called, he said, "I would like to borrow the rest of Jack Bolen's tapes."

I said, "Well you'll have to come over here and listen to them. I don't want my tapes disappearing."

That was the beginning of my relationship with Jim, to whom I have been happily married for 16 years. It was the experience in the restaurant that led me to declare consciously what I wanted for my life. I still remember writing that I wanted a man like Jack Bolen or better, and it was through Jack's tapes that I met Jim. In the restaurant scene, I remember a family behind us who were all wearing Teachings of The Inner Christ's tee-shirts with our double heart logo which states, "Love Is The Only Power." Although I didn't know that family, they were a harbinger of the truth that connected the whole experience with Jack, my friends, and most importantly, Jim with myself. Love and truth was the precipitating force behind this series of experiences which through the spirit of love led to the man whom I love so very much. Jim is not Jack Bolen, but he is the love of my life and it was love that connected us directly and indirectly. You may call it coincidence; I call it divine love and connection! *Love is the only real power on earth!*

Diane's Story
Touched by Angels

"I simply believed. I simply believed." My mother and I had been praying before I went to my room. Somehow, I knew that I had to stop thinking to get into the spirit realm. How I knew this at the age of five, I'll never know. I tried hard not to think when I asked God for a revelation. My thoughts did stop, and I heard this soft female angel voice say, "Donahue," but I didn't know what that meant. Immediately after the angel spoke, I looked at the ceiling in this non-thought space. I saw little white ringlets ascending up and disappearing, like little halos. Perhaps they were. These two experiences became the foundation for my faith – it showed me that God is real, and that He is there for me. From then on *I simply believed.*

"You dummy, what's the matter with you." My dad grabbed my arm and acted like he was going to slug me. There was so little that I could do right in my father's eyes. From my childhood into my late twenties, he was viciously intolerant of myself and my older brother. In fact he was down right abusive. I always imagined it was because my older brother and I had so little in common with him. Now I know differently.

My father was a perfectionist; everything had to be just right for him. Every day he would follow me around yelling and ordering me to do things – I had to do things his way, whatever that was at the time. And when I did it wrong, he would yell, "You know what you did. Now stop it." Then he would take his fingers and gouge my eyes. I could never figure out what I had done. I was always afraid to be in the same room, fearing that he would hurt me really bad.

I was a prisoner in my own home. My father kept certain areas of the house off limits to me. I was not allowed in the kitchen, hallway or livingroom. This was especially confusing because my sister and brothers had free access. Sometimes, my father would motion with his finger for me to go to my room. Later he would come to my room and tell me to stay there and not come out. He would say, "Don't you tell your mother I did this to you." After being in my room all day, I would sometimes try to come out, but he would simply motion with his finger for me to go back. Frequently, he made all of us children stay in our rooms lying on our beds without doing or say anything. It was like he expected us to be dead to the world.

My dad and mom argued almost every day. It was always some kind of abusive chaos happening in our house. " I'd like to stick invisible pins on the back of the kitchen door so the next time you go out the door they will gouge your eyes out" was one of his typical comments. He often threatened the whole family by saying he was going to shoot us all, then add, "especially you Diane." He'd threaten that he was going to hurt me so bad I would end up in the hospital, or " I'm going to put you in your grave." I was terrified. When I ate sometimes, he would say, "You've already eaten," grabbing my food and throw it in the sink. One time while I was eating he yelled at me and with his bare hands broke the tray stand. I remember he grabbed a lamp and tossing it to the floor. He was going to hurt me. I just knew it.

Dad's abusive behavior infected the whole family. My brothers and sister would tease me and keep secrets from me. Sometimes, they treated me as though I didn't exist. My sister ordered me around, yelling criticisms at me; at other times she was nice; I never knew what to expect. I was even teased and picked on by the kids at school. I always felt like a weird monster from another planet. I grew to despise myself.

By the time I was ten, my life was quite bizarre. Horrible things began to repeat in my mind over and over. I would sit on my bed rehashing a fantasy of different ways I wanted to kill my father. I would shoot him, pretending my finger was a gun, or stab him and kick him through the ceiling. My pain and anger became all consuming.

After long periods of painfully destroying my father with fantasies, I would be terrified. I was so afraid that I wanted to take it all back. I would begin repeating, " I'm not angry. I don't want to kill him. It didn't really happen." Using my hands, I would act like I was erasing the whole episode. In my mind I would say, everything is back to normal. I began fearing my fantasies would become real. I created a compulsive ritual to fight off the thoughts that my parents would be killed in a horrible automobile accident and that we would all go to hell.

I became a slave to strange behaviors and thoughts. I began to touch things in an secret way and a certain amount of times. When my parents were away I would run in the house stomping my foot on every pattern in the rug that was shaped like a foot. If I missed one I would have to go back and do it again. I would even have to strike my foot against lines and run up and down the stairs striking each one a certain way and for a certain amount of time. My magical number was four. I would count compulsively in fours. I remember sitting on my bed repeatedly saying the same thing, playing with my hair, and blinking my eyes while all the time rocking back and forth. I was afraid that if I didn't do these things my parents would die or get into a horrible accident.

When I was thirteen years old, all these behaviors became progressively worse. I felt that I had to carryout every thought that came to my mind. Over time, I began to stop eating and drank less. I became skinny and dehydrated. I remember feeling how nice it would be to drink a soda or how a cold glass of milk would feel, but I was a slave to my thoughts. In the summer time, I remember being so thirsty; it was a miracle that I didn't have physical complications. I became very withdrawn and depressed. I was afraid to talk, to move, to think, or to feel. I would lay on my bed or sit in a chair staring off in a daze. I was as dead as you could be and still be breathing. Something inside of me just said, "let yourself go." So I did.

When I started soiling my pants, my mother realized something was very wrong. She took me to see a psychiatrist, which only reinforced my belief that I was bad and wicked, but it also gave me a glimmer of hope – maybe he could understand and help me. He admitted me to a psychiatric hospital and by the third session, he very gently said, " It's not your fault. You were abused." Then, he said, "Do you want help?" I felt a presence come over me and a loving, gentle voice said, "Faith." Suddenly I knew that voice was Jesus. My faith bolstered by my first angel experience, and my prayers with my mother and her teachings of Jesus now solidified on a path of recovery and faith.

During my four months in the hospital, I let go and trusted Jesus to bring healing to all the painful humiliating experiences I had endured. My doctor tried several different medications and finally found one that worked for me. I attended all the group sessions and took everything one day at a time. My mother would visit me and we would pray. She reassured me that God loves me and hoped that one day I would understand the reason for all that had happened.

During my hospital stay and four years of outpatient therapy, I often wondered if I would get through all the pain and abuse. Back then, things often looked black and hopeless. The only hope I had was the feeling of the precious love of

Jesus inside me. The medication, the group and individual therapy began helping me to overcome my fears. As I started feeling more positive, I even spoke up more; my compulsion and obsessions lost their control over me as I became stronger. I learned that my father probably would never change, and I stopped trying to get his love and approval. I even learned to stand up to my father – When I yelled back that first time, he was shocked – I went to my room shaking.

Throughout high school and into my early 20s, I was able to have minimal contact with my father. I had a job in a department store. My hours were in the evening and my dad worked during the day. I was often away with my first really close friend, Eileen. We would go to the beach and parties, meeting people and having fun. Having fun was totally alien to me; I even thought that I had to pray to God for forgiveness. Now, I know that having fun is a healthy part of life.

I was 24 years old when I started having problems again. I was going through some heavy stuff at home; my dad was abusing me again. At the same time, I believe my doctor reduced my medication. I felt twisted and contorted like I was being pulled apart and at the same time dying again. My behavior must have been unusual, because at work two fellow Christian employees became aware of my condition and told me that I should see my doctor – immediately, the angel's voice of my childhood returned reiterating what my co-workers had told me. Then the presence of the Lord came over me and a gentle voice said to all three of us, "She's my child." I believe we all heard the voice!

I ignored the admonitions to see my doctor. I was stubborn and angry at God for all my Dad's abuse. I even went off my medication. As my life went down hill, I begun feeling trapped in my job. For two more years, I was a walking dead person until I was laid off. I went through some difficult mental and emotional episodes and felt almost totally abandoned by spirit, as though Jesus had left me.

Just before I was laid off, I had a deja vu experience. I was watching the Phil Donahue show and realized the name Donahue was what the angel had said when I was five years old. I had seen two of his shows where they had covered obsessive-compulsive disorder. I believed that I would have been on one of those shows had I obeyed the angel when she told me to go to my doctor. My girlfriend said that the message was probably just to reaffirm that I was not alone with my disorder, but to this day I still have the feeling that I should have been on one of those shows.

As my behavior and emotions worsened, my mother readmitted me in the hospital. There I was administered medication again and in a couple of weeks started feeling much better. A hospital social worker helped me to become more independent, so I didn't have to live with my father anymore. I felt alive again; I started attending a twelve-step program of recovery and now live in my own apartment. I've even had a speaking part in a world-famous play.

The Lord has given me a vision to help other people who are struggling to overcome abuse. I have empathy, compassion and sensitivity to those with similar backgrounds. I have gained wisdom and insight from my experiences and by walking with faith. Some may call me childish, but in terms of my life and my spiritual path, I say, " I know God is there, and I simply believe."

Serge Kahili King, Ph.D.

The Birth of a Hawaiian Shaman

'A'ohe pau ka 'ike i ka halau ho'okahi
(All knowledge is not taught in one school)

Shamanism is a definitive form of healing with Hawaiian shamanism being a distinct style within those practices. The outstanding quality of the shaman, regardless of culture, is the inclination towards engagement or creative activity. Knowledge and understanding or passive acceptance is not enough for a shaman, who plunges into life playing the role of co-creator with all the ability of mind and senses. Regardless of culture, location, or social environment a shaman's activism is, by purpose, a healer of mind, body, and circumstance. This focus towards social and environmental benefit is what distinguishes the shaman from the sorcerer of Castaneda's model who follows a path of strictly personal power and enlightenment.

Most shamans follow the "way of the warrior," whereas the Hawaiian shaman tradition follows what might be called "the way of the adventurer." A "warrior" shaman tends to personify fear, illness, or disharmony while focusing on his development of power, control, and combat skills as a means of defeating the problem. An "adventurer" shaman, by contrast, tends to depersonify these conditions i.e. treats them as effects, not things and deals with them by developing skills of love, cooperation, and harmony. For example, in dealing with a person who is emotionally upset, the two approaches might proceed as follows: The warrior shaman might help you to build a strong psychic shield to protect yourself from the other person's negative energy. In comparison, the Hawaiian shaman would be more likely to teach how to harmo-

nize your energy so that you can remain calm and thus become a possible healing source for the other person. In addition, the warrior shaman's path is often quite lonely, while
the adventurer's path, by its very nature, is quite social.
However, I have great respect for warrior shamans and their
healing. Moreover, to tell the difference between masters of
either path is difficult, if not impossible. Generally, since a
master has less to fear, his power leads to more expressions
of love, which generates more power as a corollary of his
greater confidence. Although I have walked both paths I, like
my father before me, chose the Hawaiian Adventurer tradition and method. I believe it is the most practical and beneficial, which is why I teach it today.

As a boy I had a natural openness and curiosity which my
father encouraged. When I was three years old, he taught me
to read and fostered my interests with books on adventure,
famous people and places. He had traveled extensively and
shared with me many adventurous stories about his life, all of
which stimulated my natural inclination towards exploration.
My father never fed me dogma, and even though on Mother's
side I was raised a Catholic, I never felt restricted in questioning liturgy or doctrine. In fact, I studied the history of the
early church and bible thoroughly as a way to deepen my
knowledge and understanding. To this day I continue to respect the spiritual ideas that I learned through my studies,
even though I have discarded many items as not being useful.

My father never forced or indoctrinated this liv-
ing/spiritual path on me. It was never a discipline of "only
this." Thus my father encouraged me to explore everything
from science to comparative religion, which eventually led
me to an undergraduate degree in Asian studies. Naturally
curious, I studied and researched extensively many philosophies of Asia and many world religions, which included
practicing many of their techniques and methods. Still, I al-

ways came back to the Hawaiian path because it was so simple, self-empowering, and effective, allowing me plenty of room to grow.

When I was seven years old, I had an intensely focused, profound, and enjoyable experience, which enhanced my love of the natural sciences and connected me to a deeper appreciation for the greater mystery behind everything. In the local paper was a story of a meteor shower that was supposed to be quite exceptional. Subsequently, a lot of the townspeople were talking about it, and I was very interested and excited. When the day came I could hardly contain my enthusiasm, waiting for daylight to end and the sky to grow dark. I can remember going outside to watch the little light dots shoot across the sky, as many as 100 an hour or more it seemed to me. It was quite a show!

I remember lying down on the sidewalk and just watching and watching. . .I was out there for the longest time, and don't remember ever going home. The grandeur, beauty and mystery sparked a deep resonating interest within me. What is this? What's going on? This numinous experience, engendered by awesome forces, germinated a deeper fascination with science and the scientific method while at the same time touching a mysterious and wondrous feeling within me. This beautiful nature/divine feeling and impression was the catalyst in back of many of my life's adventures.

That night I opened up to the vastness of the universe and its mystery which in some way made me larger. I established a relationship and connection with this grandeur which influenced a lifelong fascination with stars and the cosmos. In fact when I was barely in junior high, I took an extracurricular course in astronomy at the University of Michigan. I stayed up at night plotting the course of planets, which eventually almost led me to choose astronomy as a career. Still, it was the sense of the unseen mystery behind my experience and feeling that moved and awed me.

When I was 14, my father took me aside and said that it was time for me to make a choice. He told me about how he had been genuinely, but unofficially, adopted into an Hawaiian family and their traditional teachings. He offered to instruct me in this tradition and teachings, which dealt with nature, the mind, the body and many other things already of interest to me. After a period of time thinking about his offer, I went to my father and said, "Yes, I want to do this." My affirmative answer was my conscious declaration of a process that had already been laid down through my nature/divine experience along with my father's modeling and guidance in my early years.

My father gave me a piece of paper with a set of instructions or practices, and from that day forward, I was in training. This path of learning and experiencing never took place in a classroom setting, but permeated my daily life. Everything was a part of this other point of view, and since I lived on a farm, this included all the people, animals , buildings machinery, work and play.

To be in harmony, connected and aware was the message that ran through most of my father's guidance and teaching. For example, my Mother was deathly afraid of lightning, which began to negatively influence me. My father took me outside and said, "No, look at it! Look at its beauty and form; how when the light flashes, you can see the color and shape of the clouds as they come alive out of the darkness." He said, "Don't worry about being hit; you'll never know, if it hits you." Consequently, he taught me not to have fear in the presence of this awesome force of nature but to be connected through appreciation and awareness.

In our fast-paced Western lifestyles, we tend to alienate ourselves as being apart from nature. The truth is that everything we have comes from nature, which in turn comes from the divine. For example, we have a tendency to think of a building as something separate from nature; it isn't. All things come from nature and are simply reorganized into man-made manifestations, and so a building is natural because it is made up from elements of nature. Being part of nature, it has a spirit; thus, one can have a relationship with it. In fact, you are relating all the time with everything whether or not you are conscious of that fact. I know through my experiences that it is best to choose an amicable and beneficial relationship while always striving to improve what is already good.

After some time learning to be truly connected with nature, a friendly relationship can develop. In my friendship with nature I strive to fulfill nature's needs while having nature help fulfill my needs. By directing a positive intent, nature will do its best to cooperate. This can be something big that helps the environment, world and society, or it can be rather simple: " Look rain, I'm going out to my car, and I'd just as soon have you stop a few minutes." If the rain can stop, it will. If it can't stop completely , it will at least lighten up. It's not a coincidence when this happens hundreds of times in your life; it's a relationship based on friendship.

My living relationship with the animate and inanimate world is based on the assumption that everything is alive. This is a personal decision because you can't prove it. Still, we all come from the same source; everything is made up of the essence that goes into star-stuff. Based on this assumption, you can have a connection with all things, assisting in their communication and being assisted in yours. If you assume that "so-called" inanimate objects are not alive, you cut yourself off from that part of life. From a practical point of view, it makes more sense to assume aliveness in all things because it gives you greater resources and opens you up to a universe that is always communicating. We benefit when we begin to listen. We are enriched!

Now, let me illustrate this concept with an actual life experience. Of course, this experience is open to interpretation. Still for me, it is a "knowing" based on a tradition that values this "other view," and realizations born through many life experiences of this enjoyable life perspective. Not too long ago, I had been under a lot of stress; my wife, some friends and I went up to the mountains to ski and take a respite from the pressure and my heavy work load. Suddenly, I had a premonition that there was going to be an accident. My feeling and intuition was that I was receiving a forewarning message from the mountain. So I spoke to the mountain spirit: "Look, I thank for your help, but let's not have an accident. Now that I'm aware of it, we can diminish it. We can do away with it. We don't have to let this happen. So I appreciate your cooperation."

We took the lift to the top ski run about 10,000 feet high. I began to ski down the mountain with a feeling of exhilaration. Suddenly, I hit an icy area, and my skis went out of control. I was heading directly for a cliff and an exposed area with some sharp jagged rocks. My right ski stuck, and I went flying straight towards this precariously sharp rock. Everything was in slow motion, and I knew if I hit that rock I'd be ripped open from neck to groin. On my left wrist I was wearing a gold bracelet which for me had special meaning. Without thinking, I lifted my left hand to my chest and hit the rock exactly on the gold bracelet, which catapulted me in a tumbling somersault over the rock and into a patch of snow. Somewhat dazed, I felt like my wrist was broken. I laid there in the snow calling on my healing knowledge to fix my wrist.

After a period of rest, I stood up and finally went down the hill. Later, I realized that the gold bracelet was gone, and I gave it as gift to the mountain spirit while embracing the event as a sign of needed change in my stressful life. I believe the mountain spirit tried to forewarn me, and in communicating I modified and lessened the accident so that I was only shaken, not damaged.

My father died when I was 17 years old. A year and half later I was adopted into the Kahili family as was my father before me. My Hawaiian adopted grandfather placed me in his daughter's tutelage; she was now my aunt by adoption. My training intensified under her instruction because she introduced me to many different aspects of the Hawaiian knowledge and tradition. Body work, transfer of healing energy, and relationships with people and things were some of the areas she presented. For instance, Kahi Loa, a form of massage, originated from her teachings. I took the elements of what she taught and organized it with some advanced body awareness and knowledge into a seminar which we teach around the world. As a teacher of knowledge and wisdom, she was inspirational.

When I was quite young, my father told that there were individuals watching over my development. At that early age, I didn't quite understand what he meant, but in hindsight my life's journey always seemed to have someone furthering my deeper understanding of the "other view." This was true in school, the marines, and as a manager of a relief and development project in West Africa. While in Africa, I trained with an African friend of the Kahili family for about 6 ½ years. While working in the bush, he would appear at random when I least expected him. With his help I experienced some of the most adventurous years of my life. During this time my understanding of ritual, shape changing and healing was

deepened, and I was lucky to be introduced to several traditional healers who were masters with their art.

I feel blessed to have walked this path throughout most of
my life. I have tremendous gratitude for those that have
walked before me and have led the way. My life has been full
of adventure and wondrous experiences originating directly
from the shared knowledge and wisdom of my loving teachers. For through their guidance, I have opened to that which I
did not see or know. Now, I teach the path taught to me as a
blessing and appreciation to each individual who comes forward wanting to develop and learn the value of this "other
view." This "other view" is a integral part of my life, being
and experiences. In my opinion, there is nothing greater.

As a blessing to your individual journey, I share with you
our basic Aloha philosophy:

1. The world is what you think it is.

2. There are no limits.

3. Energy flows where attention goes.

4. Now is the moment of power.

5. To love is to be happy with.

6. All power comes from within.

7. Effectiveness is the measure of truth.

In closing I extend my blessing to All.

Paul Heussenstamn

Riding Life's Waves

We had been surfing all day long with the waves twice the normal size. They were great fun to ride, many curling right over my head. Riding those ocean water tubes was unbelievable. It was a surfer's paradise with our hearts filled with wave passion. Oh, those waves were great! Still, we could feel and see the signs of trouble. We kept surfing anyway.

At first, the wind didn't bother us, but as the day progressed the velocity kept increasing and the sky darkened over with clouds. Although the rain started slow, it was pouring sheets of water by the time we were packed-up and moving away from the coast. I had a squeamish feeling in my stomach. I was afraid. Trouble was brewing and we knew it!

As the wind began to howl, we drove as fast as possible towards a tiny inland village. When we reached the small one-room dwelling, I knew that we were in the teeth of a ferocious Mexican hurricane. As we unlocked the first of a two-door entrance, the door was ripped completely off its hinges and blew away into the chaos of one squall after another. Entering the room we saw frightened surfers all hunkered down for the slightest possible protection. Throughout that night the wind and rain whipped around our small structure as nails and wood groaned and creaked with the roof slowly stripped away. The noise terrified and overwhelmed me....how that building remained standing I'll never know for sure. We escaped with our lives. I shall never forget that night.

At the age of 13, I started in this very dangerous sport with a Safari surf board, a birthday gift from my parents. Little did we know at the time the many adventures surfing had in store for me. On weekends my parents would take my friend and me to the beach, and his parents would pick us up in the evening. In high school, I entered a tribe of surfers who made hitching rides easy. By the time I was a senior, I was a full-fledged member of the clan and a good surfer, as indicated by several invitations to join clubs and associations. At graduation I was fully involved in the surfing life style: I was surfing everyday, hanging out with fellow surfers, and making more money than most high school graduates working in a surf shop.

As great teachers, the ocean and surfing life were incomparable to anything I knew at the time. Up at 4:00 a.m., we would travel anywhere from Santa Barbara to Mexico exploring many different beaches for good surf, sampling their unique waves and ambiance. We lived in our swim trunks, ate good food and camped out on the beach. We would watch the sun rise and set and told surfing stories around the camp fire. I was a young man learning from other young men, and we were all connected in what the ocean taught us. Surfing completely captured my time and imagination.

My relationship with the ocean, called "The Great Mother" by the indigenous and tribal people, was as with any great teacher, based on spiritual principles and life values. As with young men in hunting tribes, her call brought together many young men of my generation to teach character, valor, courage and bravery in the timeless challenge of nature. I learned over time the many cues of external ocean forces, such as how wind, sand and swell direction affect the surf. The abundant beauty and danger associated with surfing heightened my senses and discipline, which was my introductory initiation into a direct but unconscious connection with the wisdom and spirit of my soul.

Surfing is a metaphor for life. In surfing falling is as common as traffic lights in a city. When tumbling off a surfboard, knowing the best ways to avoid injury is an important part of surfing because a wave has no sympathy when it crashes down on you. Picking yourself up and paddling out again for another wave invasion in an endless succession of chances is a lesson that easily transfers to many other life arenas.

Life never stays the same. This hard lesson is certainly taught well by the ocean; its very nature is change. A few seconds surfing the crest of a wave brings the cycle to completion as your board descends toward the beach. Looking back, the whole phenomenon that carried you has vanished. Life's cycles are always changing: up-down, in favor-out of favor, appreciated-disavowed. Surfing teaches that every wave, every moment is unique, requiring one to attune, shift and balance to a wave as well as to life's ever fluctuating themes. These skills are the very backbone of a good surfer, a well-lived life, and a spiritual journey.

The discipline to be a good surfer requires a coordination of all your sensing organs: eyes, ears, emotions, intuition, mind and body. Over time, as my skill and ability evolved, I became one-pointed while surfing. By this process the Great Mother initiated me on my spiritual journey. With the right attitude and openness to all that surfing offers, it is equivalent to or surpassing many spiritual paths. The whole surfing experience brought me to my senses and a path toward my soul.

I strongly believe that it was my destiny as a spiritual path to be in relationship to the ocean. A migratory bird doesn't need to be told when or where to fly... it's encoded in its very being. Similarly, when the ocean calls to a surfer, the response exists at the core of his being. When the surf's up and breaking good, there is a distinct feeling inside me, an electricity that permeates my house and my body...if unanswered I suffer anguish.

With the Great Mother's ocean symbolizing the unconscious, each unique ride of a wave is like a quick journey into the unknown. There are no guarantees in surfing. Every time you push off to catch a wave, you may lose your life in hundreds of different ways; being knocked unconscious and drowning is just one. Therefore a surfer's life depends on an inner alignment of the awesome external forces to one's inner resources. This is a surfer's meditation.

Becoming one-pointed through my surfing discipline was really a disguised meditation on the eternal Feminine. On a psyche level, the ocean and surfing nurtured a symbolic relationship to a deeper feminine principle within myself. This feminine principle, by its very nature, is creative and life-giving.

An array of colors and life patterns permeates throughout all the oceans living creatures: dolphins, birds and fish. Each ocean-filled day, I metaphorically felt absorbed, and imbibed the abundant life before me, deepening my connection and appreciation for the living spirit in all. An inner sensitivity grew and opened to this underlying spirit and its cycles through life. Thousands of beautiful and breathtaking sunrises and sunsets, the wonder and excitement of changing weather, and the joy of countless hours watching the Great Spirit's playful creatures unconsciously stirred and stimulated my untapped creative juices and awareness.

Surfing lit the flame to my spirituality which, in 1976, I pursued formally. Now the connection to spirit through surfing was deepened with spiritual workshops and the daily practice of transcendental meditation. I was a committed seeker searching for those that could light my way. One such individual was Krishnamurti who was a profound spiritual teacher of human thought and life principles. I often traveled to Ojai, California to hear his lectures, which frequently dazzled my thoughts and preconceived ideas about life.

Significant conflict and tension with my multimillion dollar business grew as the link and bond to my inner spirit evolved. I had started my surfing business in the back of my VW bus. With $3,000 of my own money, $5,000 dollar loan from a friend and a $10,000 loan which my uncle co-signed, I opened my first store. Within 90 days I had paid all the loans off, and within four years I had expanded to four stores, totaling sales of several million dollars. This new wealth allowed me to attend many spiritual workshops while surfing daily from my oceanfront home before going to work. Still, the business was very stressful, especially during the recession of the early '80s; the stress strengthened a desire for a balance between my inner spirit, creative nature and the strain from the business. In hindsight, big business was not my deeper path.

Continuing my formal spiritual training, I attended a two week workshop with Dr. Brugh Joy in Lucerne Valley, California. Brugh orchestrated his workshop by initiating the state of unconditional love. This state of consciousness shifts a person beyond duality and everyday perception into expanded levels of awareness and expanded levels of spiritual energy. In this deep unified state, a sense of harmony, peace, and serenity washes over you, inducing a state of clarity where the unessential aspects of personality step aside to an inclusive view of oneself and others. This unconditional love state touched me deeply as my outer persona gave way to my inner spirit.

Opened to a freer state of being and stimulated by an inner urge to create, I began drawing in my spare time. In illustrating my inner feelings and images I felt powerfully alive and connected to a deeper inner creative resource. Several months later Brugh asked me to use my workshop drawings in a line of tee-shirts. I, of course, said yes. When they began selling, my artist self-esteem soared. For the next several years, I pursued art as a hobby, taking lessons, working with an art teacher and drawing with my children.

From the time I worked with Brugh in 1979 through the next four or five years, I intensified my spiritual studies and joined a spiritual community. As a member of this community, I was given the opportunity to teach classes on a variety of spiritual concepts, techniques and forces. As a teacher I learned to fall down and get up, as I so often had surfing.

Up to this point in my life, I might have been called a "golden boy." I had learned to flow with life as one learns to ride the energy of a wave. Consequently, things usually went well, giving me the impression of invincibility. I had the Midas touch and knew it. Still, I was pursuing something bigger than personal images and successes. I was pursuing my spirituality, my soul.

Once a week I'd get up at 4:00 a.m. to drive two hours to a spiritual retreat center for meditation. My spirit quickened within the meditation group, which became profound as I deepened my own contact with unconscious forces beyond my control. In these meditations, I was moving into limitless dark voids with powerful dynamics beyond my ability to understand. I lost my inner balance, my ability to cope. I became physically sick, unable to sleep for two weeks. My life's tapestry, which I had constructed in my own image, was unraveling thread by thread right out from under me. None of my usual support systems – meditation, friends, nor my wife– were working. I was quickly losing my sense of stability as my fear increased exponentially. Everything in my life seemed void of value. Was I dying?

In small but noticeable increments everything of value began to lose its meaning as if being stripped away. My attachment to my wife, business, friends, security and spiritual disciplines were peeled back to reveal the barest of substance. I was imploding in on myself, slowly collapsing into a void lacking in anything positive. My ex-wife was helpless and baffled by what seemed to be a complete self-disintegration. In desperation I packed some bags and headed back to my spiritual community hoping for help, but they were just as bewildered as my wife. I wanted someone to help take the pain away, but I soon realized no one could...nothing I did relieved my sullen, wrenching suffering. I began slipping down deeper into an painful abyss, surrounded by a darkness that became me. I lost all hope.

After several weeks of drowning in misery, pain and darkness, I received some help from the Spiritual Emergency Network – which referred me to a therapist. He indicated that I was in the midst of the Dark Night of the Soul journey, which suggested the causes of my painful emotional and physical ordeal lay in conflicts between deeper life patterns and my everyday world . Apparently, my meditations and spiritual practices had unleashed forces that required an awesome transformation within myself. Although forces within me were demanding change, there was no individual who could guarantee my return from my pit of darkness. These forces demanded a genuine authenticity in payment for extrication from this dark hellish space. The golden boy, the Mr. Invincible, the plastic self, the material self, the foolish self had to be realigned into a new spiritual order. My life as I knew it was over. The only real question was: would I survive?

I did survive. Through grace and my willingness to eventually "let go," much stronger forces came forward into prominence within my psyche. The pain, the suffering was a crucible from which was born a deeper connection to the divine forces as they live within me. Although the golden boy image is still present within my psyche, its position of dominance had to be relinquished.

With my persona laid open and exposed, an opening emerged through my deep vulnerability which revealed more of the divine grandeur. A burgeoning authentic relationship between myself and my inner Self grew as I surrendered images that no longer provided sustenance, especially spiritually. With new eyes and perception, I saw outer reality as a shield, a mask of many images.

When I look back at the lives of famous artists, I realize that the dark night of the soul experience was common to many of them. Claude Monet is a perfect example: During one point in his life, he was distraught at his inability to sell any of his paintings. He and his wife were living a meager existence. She was sick, and he had a hard time putting food on the table. In a moment of desperation he walked over to a river and threw himself into the fast moving water. As the current pushed him down stream, the river's force and power weren't strong enough to overtake him, so he swam ashore. Instinctively, I knew what had happened to Monet. In some way he died to himself when he threw himself into the river, and the Monet that swam ashore was baptized into a greater connection to his own living spirit, to a form of divine wisdom. From that time forward, he was a different Claude Monet.

Although it took several years to integrate my dark night of the soul experiences, I knew that my outer life was out of alignment with a deeper spiritual aspect. In retrospect, I know that the bridge between my business life and my spiritual life had collapsed. I had to have a new direction in order for me to be authentic and true to myself. This authenticity, this truth came through my artistic ability to reveal the invisible, the secret language of the soul.

Four years after the dark night of the soul experience, I began painting mandalas, which are an integrated image of wholeness and symbolize the sacred center in many traditions . In the Tibetan view of life they believe that everything in an individual's life comes from the inside to the outer reality – everything. The mandala is an artistic image within present time symbolizing the many forces within the soul's unity and journey. Through sacred image, color and design the painting of mandalas helped me contact my soul's essence. As I painted mandalas, I realized that these images were helping to integrate the diverse forces within myself. Through awareness of my soul's forces, I was better able to balance and harmonize my relationship with people, projects, and goals.

The mandala deepened my spiritual journey with a connection to my own spiritual essence, a creative basic nature. Soon after the mandala images began to express themselves through me, my outer world began to fall apart. Through pain and suffering, I entered into the artist's life. My business was gone, my wife and I divorced, and she and my children were living in another home. I went kicking and screaming all the way and was left with surfing and my connection to spirit expressed through art in the form of a personal mandala.

The personal mandala is a reflection of the divine as its spiritual forces are played out in an individual life, captured in a moment of time. When I began painting personal mandalas, I immediately had several commissions. Brugh Joy bought my first painting, and Barbara Streisand wanted the second. For the next five months I toured the country talking about mandalas, and at the end of that time I had commissions for a year's work with a waiting list that grew to one then two years long.

In successive degrees my life's pilgrimage has moved into a deeper relationship with the essence of my soul. Surfing the ocean connected me to the divine Mother unconsciously, my spiritual practices made formal this connection, but it wasn't until the gut-wrenching collapse of my persona images through the dark night of the soul experiences that a volitional link to an inner spirit was assured.

The symbolic language of the soul is rich in its ability to carry vast amounts of information, awareness and knowledge as contrasted to the linear, logical, and rational way we think in the everyday world. The soul is concerned with life patterns, energies, forces, and the external nature of reality. It's the theme and motif that runs behind an individual's outer concerns and is often best expressed and understood through the wide lens of images, symbols, and themes of our sleeping dreams.

My soul connection has taught me how to read, perceive and appreciate the dynamism that is orchestrating behind the outer reality of an individual. Like radar, radio waves or e-mail, I energetically ride the wave of an individual's soul, which I symbolically represent through a personal mandala painting. My own connection and relationship to spirit is my doorway through which my soul's eyes scan the very essence, temperament, pattern, nature and quality of an individual. When I'm in my soul's awareness, the link between my soul and the soul of the person I'm painting dissolves into a confluence similar to when two rivers merge. Their energetic-spirit wave filters through my soul and is intuitively represented through shapes, colors, patterns, and forms. An individual is known at his deepest essence through soul access. In my opinion all the great master artists live in some way through their souls' mythology with the truth of this inner feeling being their guide to the material world. Cezanne said it best, "The artist is just a hypersensitive tuning fork."

Bringing people into a closer relationship with their soul is my spiritual service and path. I am deeply committed to my soul's journey, especially the balance and harmony created through the individual expression of spirit and soul as manifested in art, such as with a personal mandala. Art is a great doorway to the mystery behind the everyday reality, a doorway full of images and symbols of the soul's mystery and spirit.

Bella Karish's Story
I Lost My Voice to Find My Voice

Introduction

Author's note: An introduction to Edgar Cayce's life is important to fully understand the Bella Karish story. Edgar Cayce is recognized as one of the greatest clairvoyants the world has ever known.

As a boy, Cayce had difficulty in school with his lessons. A daydreamer, he loved reading and studying the Bible. One day he overheard a church elder say that he read the Bible completely through each year, so Cayce decided to read the Bible from beginning to end for each previous year of his life and then for each year of his life thereafter. He carried his Bible continuously reading at every possible moment. He built himself a little lean-to out of branches and reeds in the woods, a place of his own for reading the Bible.

By his thirteenth year, he had read through the Bible twelve times and was in his lean-to reading the book of Manoah when he felt a presence. Looking up he saw a woman with a shadow shaped like wings standing before him. In melodious voice she said, "Your prayers have been heard. Tell me what you would like most of all so that I may give it to you." Overwhelmed, Cayce could hardly speak but, with a voice full of trepidation and awe, he said, "Most of all I want to be helpful to others, especially children when they are sick."

At school the next day, Cayce's teacher, his Uncle Lucian, asked him to spell "cabin". Cayce's difficulty with school was reflected in his inability to even spell this word. Later that same day, Uncle Lucian apparently told Cayce's father about his son's poor academic performance. Cayce's father was very ashamed of him and kept him up to 11: 00 P.M. studying his spelling lessons. All the studying that evening was in vain. Cayce's spelling answers were still wrong. His father was so upset he knocked Cayce out of his chair twice. As Cayce was getting up for the second time, he heard inside himself the words of the lady he had seen the day before. She said, "If you can sleep awhile, we can help you." Cayce was able to convince his father for a rest and dozed off with his spelling book under his head. Amazingly, from that day forward, he could remember anything in a book so long as he first slept on it. Cayce then began to advance in school quickly and became the subject of much gossip.

One day he was hit on the spine while playing ball. For the rest of the day his behavior was quite out of the ordinary: He threw spit wads and acted out at school. He threw things at the dinner table and made fun of his father until he was sent to bed. His parents were quite worried and when he fell asleep he began to talk in his sleep saying that he was suffering from shock due to the injury of his spine; then he gave instructions for a poultice to be placed at the back of his head. Knowing that the items in the poultice were harmless, his confused parents decided to do what he said. The next morning he was fine.

Several years later Cayce was in Elkton as a traveling salesman. After suffering severe headaches for several weeks, he went to a doctor, who gave him a powder to take with a glass of water. Swallowing the dose at the hotel was the last thing Cayce remembered before waking up in bed at home in Hopkinsville, two doctors anxiously overlooking him. He could hardly talk, his voice a faint whisper. After several weeks, many doctors and specialists were unable to help, so out of desperation Cayce turned to Mr. Hart, a traveling showman-hypnotist. Under hypnosis Cayce's voice was fully restored, but he still couldn't talk when brought out of the trance. Before having to leave town, Hart tried several more times without success. Mr. Layne, the only hypnotist in town, hypnotized Cayce following the advice of Dr. Quackenboss, who suggested that while under a trance Cayce be told to discuss his own case. It worked! Casey diagnosed the problem and prescribed a treatment that successfully restored his voice. The next day Layne put Cayce in a trance and asked him to give a diagnosis and treatment for a stomach problem he had, which doctors hadn't been able to cure. Again, over time Cayce's treatment was successful! Although it took some time before Cayce was fully involved in giving readings for the sick, this was indeed the beginning of Cayce's work as the sleeping prophet, as he was later known.

Bella Karish's Story
I lost My Voice to Find My Voice

My name is Bella, and I am the president of the Fellowship of Universal Guidance. I channel wisdom teachings and help individuals with specific life situations and actions. We channel wisdom and understanding from the Eternal Cosmos or simply E.C. which comes from the banding of the Edgar Cayce teachings. This banding of particular teachers and guides transmit their wisdom through Eternal Cosmos. We deliver this wisdom through our oracle circles, the three selves evaluations and individual counseling sessions. Since 1960 we have helped many people through our work and service.

This wonderful spiritual gift of wisdom and guidance from the spiritual realm has not always been a direct part of my life. I often tell people that I was quite square until I was 40 years old. Even though my life started out quite ordinary, I have had many fascinating experiences.

I was born in Los Angeles in 1910 at the Queen of Angels Hospital. My brother and I were involved in the motion pictures in our youth. Being two years younger, he usually played a baby and I a child. When I was about nine years old, we lived directly across the street from the Mack Sennet Studios. I became very intrigued with movie stars, like Charlie Chaplin, Mabel Norman, etc. One day my brother and I crawled under the studio gates near the stage to watch the action. The stage was one big wheel and fascinating to watch. The director became furious and said, "get those kids out of here," but Mabel Norman said, "Oh no, they can stay. I'll take care of them; they'll be under my supervision." After that she used to invite me into her dressing room; she would talk to me and I listened with awe. Watching everything on and off stage, I learned a great deal.

Years later, I even baby-sat for Tomasina, the daughter of cowboy actor Tom Mix. When I was 16, I became an extra. In one film I wore a wig and played an old lady. What a sight – a teenager with gray hair.

My mother was close to Louis Meyer of Metro Goldwyn Meyer and his wife, and Charlie Chaplin once wrote about a place where actors could get sandwiches and odds and ends – that's the little store my mother owned. A picture of where she worked was in one of the comedy books, and my picture was in a magazine standing next to one of the actors.

My mother used to say, "Anyone can play the piano." So at the age of eight I started my musical training by playing the cello. I still remember carrying that heavy cello over the hill for lessons at my teacher's house. It was as big as I was.

To help my mother, I worked for the Los Angels Mirror Times, delivering a well-known writer's finished work to the Times for printing. When I was 19, I sold apples on the steps of the Federal building at the beginning of the depression.

My future husband proposed to me just after we had left a group of friends. He said, "If you don't say yes, someone else will. Will you marry me?" Because I was 24, and afraid that I would be an old maid, I married him. Not long after his proposal, we moved back to Chicago to live with his family. I really suffered there. The Chicago weather can easily dip to 20 degrees below zero, and I had never even seen snow in all my years of living in Southern California – it was a total shock to my system. Besides, his family was not happy with our living with them, so returning to sunny California was a great joy and relief.

After our two children were born, I began performing with the Women's Symphony Orchestra. We often played in quartets and trios, filling our house with exquisite sounds of music. My husband, who also played cello, enjoyed the music and fellowship when he could get away from his very busy work schedule. During this time, my mother helped by taking care of my babies until she was unable.

Later, my husband finally required that I help him in the his business, which ended my affiliation with the symphony. A great loss. My husband was a bill collector and sent me out to collect milk bills from the poor. I definitely was not happy helping him, but I did it to keep peace in our house.

After numerous separations – whereby my ex-husband would simply walk out – we separated for the final time, ending 16 years of marriage. I can still remember that Christmas Day when we were supposed to have dinner with his family and never did. I had the feeling he was involved with the lady he finally married, so in 1949 I divorced him.

My future look bleak and uncertain. Shortly after the divorce, I lost my job and was facing a serious operation because I had lost my voice and was hardly able to speak. "Strangulated throat," was what one of the doctors called my ailment. He said the cause was severe stress and emotional upset. The suggested operation required my throat muscles to be surgically loosened, which caused me more anxiety, for I was still responsible for the care of my children.

In the midst of all of this turmoil my best friend Bertha and I traveled to Northern California to the Asilomar Conference grounds for a seminar on Edgar Cayce. At the conference they spoke about Edgar Cayce's astounding psychic abilities and the events that led up to them. Bertha and I were thoroughly fascinated and excited by all that we had learned about psychic phenomena.

When we returned home, Bertha and I went to see an hypnotist who used regression and guided imagery to help people. I was one of four people picked out of the audience to be hypnotized. Under hypnosis and using guided imagery, he directed me to go inside a cave where he said I would find part of my problem. I refused. Then, he brought me out of the trance stating, " this woman has a psychological problem, and I won't attempt anything further today, but tonight she'll have a dream indicating why she wouldn't go in the cave."

That night I did have a dream and inside the cave was my husband waiting to hit me over the head with a spiked club. Obviously, my "strangulated throat" problem was related to stress and strong emotions regarding my separation and divorce from my husband.

Next came an event that changed my life completely. Bertha and I wanted to see if through channeling we could find out more about what had happened to my voice. First, Bertha tried to reach the spirit domain but nothing happened. Then I put my hand on hers and suddenly the Edgar Cayce voice came through me and said, " I'VE BEEN WAITING FOR YOU!" I was absolutely overwhelmed; except for the lecture Bertha and I attended at Asilomar, I didn't even know who Edgar Cayce was.

In hindsight I remember experiences that foretold my ability to channel. For instance, I would be walking on the street and see something that no one else could see. What's more, I could talked about things that I knew nothing about and when people would say, "where did you learn that?" I would say, "I don't know." I was already channeling without even knowing it. I soon began expecting these things to happen, despite the fact I didn't really understand them.

After the Edgar Cayce voice came through me, Bertha and I went to Los Angeles to see Peter Ballbush who had spoken at the Asilomar conference. He immediately recognized my voice as being the strangulated voice of Cayce and invited me to his meetings with the Theosophy group on Beechwood Drive, where I became the major Edgar Cayce channel; however the Cayce family did not accept that I was channeling their father's pattern of teachings. They ostracized both myself and Peter. When Hugh Lynn Cayce, the son of Edgar Cayce, came to see us, he said, "No one can be in my father's image, or be the voice of my father unless they can tell me certain things that his father only knew." I was not involved with that kind of thing, so Hugh Lynn simply ignored us and never came back. This greatly upset Peter.

I met Wayne Guthrie at Peter's group, the Brotherhood of Universal Guidance, where I stayed for a number of years. Wayne and I had a lot in common and became very good friends. Wayne was an excellent metaphysician in his own right, having had studied for many years. Wayne was nearly always present at our closed meetings where I channeled wisdom teachings as we do now and when our meetings were open to the public I channeled for individuals.

Wayne and I learned a great deal from Peter who was a wonderful teacher, leader, and guide. Unfortunately, he began using hypnosis to control the minds of the channels to communicate what he wanted said. We felt that this was negative and evil, opposite to the Christ energy. One day he was talking through Bertha, controlling her thoughts. Wayne and I were horrified because we knew that was not Bertha talking; it was Peter talking through her. Wayne and I got up and said, "Sorry Peter me cannot be a part of what you're doing." Wayne, Bertha, and I simply walked out. We did not want to be controlled by his particular actions.

After leaving, Wayne and I started the Fellowship of Universal Guidance. I was unemployed and Wayne had just left his job. At first we struggled financially with the Fellowship being our only source of income. Still, it was such a wonderful and important endeavor that we dedicated and committed ourselves to what became primarily important, this work. Helping people is our commitment to the teachers and the Fellowship. To be totally involved and totally forget self is what makes our commitment work.

I am grateful and blessed for this gift of spirit, constantly saying a prayer of thanks for being given this great gift. It is so precious, so beautiful that I am grateful to the sources that have kept me attuned with wisdom and truth. As I channel I sit just outside my body and to the left of my head. Although I can see Edgar Cayce, I don't know what Eternal Cosmos looks like. E.C. was offered as a teacher and guide personality because the Cayce family would not have allowed me the use of his name.

Sometimes when the truth is offered from the teachers through Eternal Cosmos, it is not always accepted. The truth is not always what people want to hear. The sub-conscious is the memory bank of our past lives and is given by our teachers through E.C. We must realize that we ask, choose and commit to our life occurrences to transform karma into dharma. But often as human beings we feel we don't like our circumstances and protest even when the truth about our own karmic patterns are revealed. When people become angry, distressed, and sometimes leave, I can only beg, seek and accept that my teachers tell the truth and only the truth for the highest good of all.

Over the years and so very gently, I have changed and grown with spiritual understanding and wisdom, often not even realizing that I was changing. When I was young and throughout all of my marriage I wasn't very spiritual. I simply believed that there was a God and his angels.

As a child, my mother was a practicing Orthodox Jew very bound by Jewish tradition. I remember that she kept the tradition of separate kitchen dishes for different kinds of foods like dairy and meat, but her diligent efforts faded quickly when she began working at a restaurant; it was simply impossible to keep Kosher. Besides, we had an Irish nanny who used the dishes interchangeably; the dishes became so mixed-up that my mother finally relinquished the tradition all together. Working and rearing children, my mother slowly moved from orthodox to reform to where tradition wasn't as important. She became much more open and even let us children go to our friends' for Christmas. This released me from a single spiritual point of view, but any spiritual feelings I did have were closed off during my 16 years of marriage, because my husband was so anti-religious, and I didn't want to offend him.

Now I believe that I've been guided, helped and given the greatest gift of channeling Being a spiritual person through the great creative source, I believe in all religions and all spirituality. We have been every religion in the perfect past, and we are every religion now. We are all one, no matter what the appearance.

Spirituality is a state of mind, not a particular action.. You can believe yourself to be spiritual and shout it from the housetops, and it might not mean a thing. But activated, true spirituality follows the Christ principle of loving thy neighbor as thy self. It is an active participation at the source of all creation, with God, the Sources. God has many faces and is many faceted. God is anything and everything; God is personal , male and female or a mass collective, if you want It to be. Whatever you want to choose, to do or to expect.

I want to make it clear that I'm an instrument for the teachers, guides, and Eternal Cosmos. They have changed the wisdom and knowledge in a way that it can be of help to people without my having to add my two cents. I can help people as long as I continue to believe and know that *the teachers do it.* My life pattern was chosen before I ever entered this plane. Here I really had no choice. The teachers waited for me in my subconscious mind which I now know to be true and final. I simply became affiliated as an instrument of spirit. And that has become my job and my joy.

My freedom is working with the teachers and spirit to help people. My cage was leading a life devoid of spiritual contact. I truly lost my voice to find my voice, *my spiritual voice.*

Postscript

I thought that it might be informative if I include the Prayer of Protection that we use before Oracle circles, counseling sessions, and three selves work. Also, I have included how a typical Oracle Circle channeling session would start as to acquaint the reader with our work.

Father Mother – God,
I ask that we be cleared and cleansed
Within the Universal
White Christ Light,
The green healing Light,
And the purple transmuting Flame.

Within God's Will
And for our highest good,
I ask that any and all
Negative evil energies
Be completely sealed
In their own Light,
Encapsulated within
The Ultra-Violet Light,
Cut off and removed from us.

Impersonally,
With neither love nor hate,
I return all negative evil energies
To their source of emanation,
Decreeing that they never again
Be allowed to reestablish themselves
Within me or anyone else
In any form.

I now ask that we be placed
Within a triple electro-magnetic
Shield of the Universal
White Christ Light of Protection
And for this Blessing, I give thanks.
Amen

Now we call forth Eternal Cosmos, E.C. I ask for truth and only truth for the highest good of all concerned. Let it be. At this point, I enter in peace and with love for each one for all of you have come in to this period of time, to this life time to be part of that which is helpful and brings about the good that is necessary for the planet to experience. Some of you have not truly yet understood the importance of your purpose but that too shall come into focus as time goes on and as you learn to understand your teachers, your guides, and the direct importance of your whole familiar energies which are part of the past, the present, and very much involved with your future. We will start to the right this time and we will be carefully to remember to speak up. I'm sorry if this channel seems to have trouble; I do not but she does so we will cater to her. Will you please begin?

"E.C. this is William."

"Welcome William."

"I want to know…."

Our oracle circle typically begins in a similar manner, with introductory remarks from E.C., followed by each in attendance asking one question and receiving an answer.

Michael D. McCarty's Story

The Unknown Quest

It was a trip that literally changed my life.

Let me start out by saying that before this trip I thought of myself as irreligious and aspiritual. Although I had been raised in a Catholic family and even was an altar boy, I had long ago rejected religion because of the hypocrisy in the church. I found the same hypocrisy in any religion I had come into contact with. I was an agnostic. God didn't bother me and I didn't bother with Him.

From Chicago I stopped in San Francisco to visit my friend Dave. During the couple of weeks I stayed with him, I told him of my plans to travel in the far East including India. He became excited and said that if I was going to India I should read *Autobiography of a Yogi*. At that time in my life, I didn't want anything to do with God, especially reading about Him. Nonetheless, I started reading it. Why ? I don't know. I became totally fascinated, continuing to read it while traveling from San Francisco to Hawaii and on to Hong Kong, where I finished the book.

When I finished the book, I thought maybe I could meet one of these guru guys while traveling in India. I bought another book by Yogananda, *Man's Eternal Quest*, and then met an Australian woman in Bali who loaned me of one of the Seth books. I bought a copy of it on a layover in Singapore on my way to Thailand. I kept reading similar books and when I arrived in Sri Lanka to take a an acupuncture course, I met a woman who was a follower of Sai Baba. She told me stories about how he healed the sick, raised the dead, and was able to be in more than one place at the same time.

When I went into her room for the first time, I was taken aback by a picture of Sai Baba on an altar. He had an Afro and was wearing an orange robe. I wondered, what's the deal, who is this brother and why is she praying to him? As we talked, the woman told me some more about him and where in India his ashram was located.

After the course, I went to India for decidedly non-spiritual purposes – to score some good hash and ganga. Once there, I felt drawn to Bangalore, where the woman had told me Sai Baba was staying. I decided to go and check him out. The closer I got, the more excited I became. I checked into the hotel in Bangalore and went to their bookstore to get a book on this Baba guy. There were none to be found. I ended up in an employee-only section going to a shelf moving back some things and reaching back to find the only book on Baba they had. It was full of stories about how he had changed many people's lives and performed miracles, which I found fascinating.

I went to his ashram Prashanti Nilayam, which means the abode of the highest peace. After I settled in, I went with people who came from every part of the world for darshan, which means viewing a holy man. That's exactly what I wanted to do; make eye contact with this Sai Baba guy. When he came out , he walked around taking letters and talking to individuals; then out of thousands of people he walked directly over to me and looked me right in the eyes. I was overwhelmed. At that moment I knew Sai Baba was whoever he said he was.

At darshan, Baba invited me to an interview the next morning. I had no idea of the real significance, but I had the feeling something wonderful would happen. I didn't having a clue as to what. Somebody said, "oh yeah, go for the interview." This spurred me on and increased my excitement.

In the interview room, Baba was sitting with about twelve people just looking at us when suddenly he started a circular motion with his hands and out of the air began to materialize objects. He raised his hand and pulled up his sleeve as though to silence the skeptics. Then, while he made a vertical circle with his hand, a Jappa Malla, an Indian rosary of 108 beads, popped out of mid-air a foot away from his hand. I was totally blown away and amazed that he was able to share about individuals connected to people in the room without even knowing them as confirmed by the expressions on their faces and heads nodding in agreement.

I was then given a private interview with Baba. He began to talk about my life, not in vague generalities but with specific names and details of specific incidences. He talked about things that only I could know. He was all up in my business. At the time of the interview, I was an acupuncturist who was detoxing drug addicts and at the same time selling drugs on the side. I believed in job security. I was also into a lot of other negative things like drugs, women, and orgies. Baba made it clear that he would help me. He said there was too much lust in my life. "Sometimes you want to be with Mary – my girlfriend – and, at times, with all those other women." He told me not to worry about things like money, health, or career that he would take care of it all. Now, I was truly blown away!

In a later interview, I realized that Baba had helped me before I had ever met him. He shared with me an incident with my then girlfriend in the early 1970s. She and I had gone to a New Years Eve party and had had a bad argument. She took a cab home and I came home later, choosing to sleep on the couch. In the middle of the night, I heard this voice say, "wake up." I woke up but couldn't move or open my eyes. This voice said, "Pretend like you're asleep and turn over and take a peek." I could now move my body again.

What had happened to momentarily paralyze my body? Where had the strange voice originated? I felt compelled to followed its instruction. When I turned over pretending to be asleep, I saw my girlfriend coming towards me with a 30 caliber carbine, obviously about to send me to a much closer relationship with God. Next Baba spoke about how the voice had saved me another time when my girlfriend was going to pour hot Crisco on me. I then knew that he had been that Voice.

I was a changed person after I left Baba's ashram. My life could never be the same. Unfortunately, part of me wanted to reject my experiences with Baba; I still had a very wild nature. Sitting on the balcony of my hotel room, I felt overwhelmed and confused. I literally didn't know what to do. I'll smoke a joint, that will calm me down. As I rolled the joint, I glanced into the sky. There from the ground to beyond the clouds appeared the image of Sai Baba in his orange robe and large Afro staring directly at me. I dropped the joint. Then I saw the image of Christ and other beings looking at the image of Baba. I felt shock, wonder and awe!

I thought of the pornographic magazines I kept for my pleasure, and because I could sell them for lots of money in that part of the world. I tore them all up into little pieces. Whereas I had been looking for all kinds of sexual encounters, I now was avoiding them. The original stuff that was of interest to me became unimportant.

When I returned home, I became celibate and stopped certain parts of my drug involvement. At one point I tried to stop all of my negative activities. I stopped dealing; I stopped getting high I became celibate. But my faith was not strong enough and after a month I went back to dealing because that was the way I made my living. I also went back to smoking grass but stopped indulging in cocaine.

In 1983 I went back to see Baba. He told me that my willpower was weak. Although he didn't refer to drugs directly, I knew what he meant. It was not easy to give up selling drugs; I was used to making lots of money. I read one of Baba's stories that inspired me about a man who wanted to stop drinking but couldn't. Baba told him to drink as much as he wanted but to dedicate every drink to him. Over time the man was able to stop drinking. When I return to Chicago, I thought, *okay every time I smoke a joint or sell a package I'll dedicate it to him.* But I had very little actual faith, because I wanted to accumulate a bankroll before I stopped.

I had always been practical when it came to my security. I should have been making lots of money, but it was like money was going up in smoke. After awhile, I knew the meaning of this indirect message and decided on January 18, 1984, to quit. I owed several people money. So first, I called the guy to whom I owed several thousand dollars. I told him that I didn't know when or if I would be able to pay back the money to him, but I couldn't sell drugs anymore. To my astonishment, he said, okay forget about the money. This was not the way I thought this would come down, but in fact everyone I owed money either dropped it or allowed me to trade art, stereo equipment, or something else for the debt. I was out of the business.

When I left the drug business in 1984, I moved into a small apartment with nothing but a card table and a couple of pillows for furniture. I was living on the economic edge. Once, my rent was late; my car payment was due; and I had no money with no prospects of getting any. I really began to worry, then I remembered that Baba told me not to worry. So I just let it go and went to bed. Sleeping was one way I avoided worrying.

About one in the morning, a friend called. At the beginning of our conversation, she asked if I needed any money and how much. I told her; she said, come over in the afternoon and get a check. She not only gave me the money for my immediate bills, but she also gave me a job doing janitorial work. Although I was known for hating to get dirty, I was still grateful for this job that provided me with enough to get by. When I needed something, somehow it was provided.

I wanted to go to Baba's 60th birthday celebration which included a world conference, but I had no money. A woman I had met on my first trip wrote and said I deserved to be at such an auspicious occasion. She said just take care of the arrangements, and the money will come. Don't worry.

Things began to happen. I found some money on the street to pay for my Visa; I was hired to paint an office that nobody used; and friends in my former drug business helped me out after they had heard about my plans. It was amazing. I ended up at the ashram with thirty dollars in my pocket; I spent three months in India, a month in Taiwan and returned to Los Angeles with eighteen dollars. I never wanted for a thing the entire time I was gone.

Although a second incident ended positively, it was not quite as pleasant. When I returned to Los Angeles, I stayed with a friend who had made it clear that she could only tolerate me for a few days and at the most a week. I had been there a month and things were very tense. I tried to stay out of her way, which was difficult. In her crazy apartment, I had to go through her bedroom to get to any of the other rooms. The washroom, located in her bedroom, was particularly troublesome considering I had to make plenty of trips because of my prostate problem. I was on pins and needles most of the time I was there.

One evening, I was feeling unwanted as I walked back to my friend's apartment after attending a Sai Baba meeting in Hollywood. I had known no one at the meeting, which augmented my bad case of the blues. I was literally walking with my head down when a piece of paper fluttered through the air and landed at my feet. I glanced at it and it read, *smile God loves you.* I started laughing. I said, "Okay Lord, I've been trying to find work and a place to stay. If you want me here you are going to have to hook me up."

Things began to happen again. Within a week I had another place to stay, two weeks later I had a job, and a month later a perfectly good car that I bought for one dollar. It just happened, happened, happened. That's the way my life goes.

I have to keep in mind who I have become compared to who I was. Shortly after I met Baba, I realized my life was going to be different. I remember being in my hotel room after my first visit writing down these words: *This is amazing ; this is unbelievable; this is the task I always dreamed of, the spiritual rejuvenation of humanity. I still shudder when I think of those words. I know my part of it is to improve myself while helping others. I know as I change it affects those* around me. I remember seeing one of my former drug buddies on the street.

He said, " Let's get high, I have some good herb."

I told him that I didn't get high anymore. His mouth dropped open.

He said , "Wow if you don't get high anymore, maybe I should stop too."

That's the way it goes; we all have an affect on each other!

Brugh Joy, M.D.

The Medicine of Initiation

Life is the great crucible for initiation. In this stirring pot is placed all that is needed to transform and heighten the individual soul towards awareness of a broader and deeper perspective. My whole life is a continuous series of initiations. Sometimes I dread when another layer opens up because the consequences are nearly always uncomfortable. As the old perspectives, images, and forms break apart, I am vulnerable to the unfamiliar ground coming into my awareness. Still, there can be no turning away from the pursuit of these new unfolding expansions if one is to honor self-realization.

Initiations are the passageways that move us into newly developing arenas. They are easily recognizable in the structure and order of social communities. Joseph Campbell in *Myths to Live By* states it well: "Myths are the mental supports of rites; rites, the physical enactment of myths. By absorbing the myths of his social group and participating in its rites, the youngster is structured to accord with his social as well as natural environment and turned from an amorphous nature product, prematurely born, into a defined and competent member of some specific, efficiently functioning social order." In our society we see passage and initiation examples in the marriage and commencement ceremony, and in the simple act of getting a driver's license, which is a major coming of age initiation.

Initiation can also be the rending of beliefs and perspectives that no longer serve the inherent development within a particular individual. This is most often seen in its simplest form through "the aha experience" which shifts awareness on a particular point or topic. In its most dramatic form, initiation can collapse an entire belief system, opening an individual to bigger and grander perspectives, usually accompanied by a richer connection to one's own spirit. These life changing initiations transform the direction and character of one's life. Transformational events of this kind often seem fixated at a particular crossroads in life but really are gleaned through many years of personal development.

All systems of belief rest on hypothetical foundations. We all start out entrapped in hypotheses that have been constructed into absolute truths. When transformation arrives, we see that our absolute truths are only temporary structures capable of teaching only relative truths, and as a consequence these relative truths are only valid in the context of their organizing ideation.

Transformation enlarges the context of reality. One's awareness is lifted up into states of consciousness where the multidimensional nature of existence is perceived, not just conceived; where it is experienced, not just imagined; where each dogma and each absolute truth is seen as but a single facet of a superconscious whole called Beingness. In the totality of Beingness there is no absolute anything – no rights or wrongs, no higher or lower aspects – only the infinite interaction of forces, subtle and gross, that have meaning only in relationship to one another. Absolutes are concoctions of our rational mind. Reality must never be confused with concoctions. The Transformational Process, the release from fixed beliefs, allows the fragmented awareness to meld into universality.

My mother laid the foundation for my openness to the principles behind life's universality and wholeness. In her daily life, I easily observed the respect she held for all life forms. She removed small creatures and insects outdoors with care and ease and talked to plants and flowers with a deeply felt love.

She believed in the harmony behind everyday life, respecting those teachers and teachings that sought harmony's value and meaning. Mother and I had endless long discussions on metaphysical realms, sharing creative insights, visions and conflicts. She fostered and welcomed spiritual exploration and learning in general while at the same time nourishing my sensitive and aesthetic values through harmony in music, the arts and deeper spiritual values.

Unusual for the time, Mother's openness to eclectic spiritual beliefs and practices nurtured my insight and creativity, allowing a space for my many intuitive flashes of future events, which were always prophetic, signaling major changes, usually years in advance. One such intuitive flash happened in my late teens before I entered college to commence the prerequisites for medical school. It implied clearly that I wouldn't be practicing medicine after the age of thirty-five.

Long before the actual events, my awareness signaled change from life patterns as yet not even begun. Perceiving future events, even if only partially, fit well into my mother's conviction that time was just a belief system and not of universal importance. Past, present, and future were simply concepts of a time-based reality. Conversely, awareness and consciousness provide the ability to explore and operate in all time's dimensions or even in timeless realms. This fluidity available through consciousness allows for past events to be corrected just as well as present circumstances. As an absolute truth about reality, time's sequential and chronological display of life events was shattered with my many intuitive flashes about future events in my life.

As if an afterthought of my higher state of Beingness, I did pursue medicine as a career and was quite successful both within academia and as a physician. I was elected to Alpha Omega Alpha, the medical school honor society. My internship and first year of internal medicine residency was at the Johns Hopkins Hospital. The final two years of internal medicine residency was at the Mayo Clinic in Rochester, Minnesota. I was a Fellow of the American College of Physicians and the American College of Chest Physicians. I was commended for my service at Balboa Naval Hospital in San Diego. I was on the staff of Good Samaritan Hospital and an assistant clinical professor of medicine at the University of Southern California while at the same time enjoying a growing practice in Los Angeles.

During my medical school training all of my psi abilities stopped as if someone had turned off the paranormal spigot. As an undergraduate, I often had been able to intuit an exam the night before or allow answers to exam questions to simply flow into my awareness even if I hadn't studied the related area of information. Later, I realized that loss of my psi-abilities was the catalysis that forced the greater development of my intellectual capabilities. I studied with enthusiasm the interesting complexities of the human body.

At age twenty-seven, my intuition began to trickle back into my awareness. During my residency at the Mayo Clinic, I had another intuitive flash that I would meet and study with a woman spiritual teacher in Los Angeles, California in my early thirties. By the time I finished my internship at the clinic, my intuition was flowing freely again, which rekindled my interest in metaphysics and higher states of consciousness.

When I finally met Eunice Jean Hurt in December 1971, I was swept into a state of ecstasy by the pure radiance of her

Beingness, which was Love made manifest. In a little less than 11 months, she had completely transformed all my skepticism and defenses about higher states of consciousness. Her ability to blend with heightened and expanded portions of her Beingness was a remarkable transformation to watch. In a blink of her eye, she was a different entity, saint-like, whose words were like liquid light, and whose presence was sheer mana. Instantaneously, she demonstrated a Christ consciousness – the essence of Love.

In the nine months prior to her death, she took a few of her students into realms I had only read about. For the first time, through the induction of her presence, I experienced Unconditional Love. The radiance of her Unconditional Love touched the essence of my Beingness, connecting me to the state of Divinity that resides in everyone. Unconditional Love is non-judgmental, non-emotional, non-sexual and non-mental; yet conveys the warmth, peace, and joy of the Divine Ambrosia while melting individuality into an inner connection to universal relationship. This was her great gift, a gift that runs through my body, mind, soul – my very essence.

On a late November morning in 1972, Eunice died. It was a deep personal loss.

Eunice had given the gift of a lifetime and I knew it, but now continued self-awareness was my responsibility and no one else's. I knew the path was internal, and there could be no further external teachers. Eunice had awakened my spirit to a path and vista that had deeply moved me; continuing on the journey was vital to who I was.

Almost two months after Eunice's death, I found my Inner Teacher who was my direct link to wisdom and knowledge beyond my learning, understanding and experiences. My awareness was now guided to many significant insights: The presence of body energy fields; the ability to scan the body for disease and transfer healing energy into it, the detection of a more elaborate chakra system and the ability to balance it energetically.

I began to integrate and demonstrate these powerful alternative healing practices with my patients and selected colleagues. As a respected member of the fraternity, my hope was to create a momentum for change from within the medical community. However, lingering just below the surface of my life's everyday concerns and my responsibilities as a physician was the intuitive impress that happened over a decade ago, prior to even entering my academic training. As you recall it revealed that I would not be a practicing physician after my 35th birthday.

On January 27, 1974, I turned 35 with some trepidation, but the day came and went with no extraordinary revelations or insights. By the end of the day I had completely rationalized away any significance to the whole idea of ending my career as a physician. As a respected doctor, I felt I could influence conventional medicine the easy way from the inside. Besides, my life as a physician with all its privileges, esteem and security was profoundly enjoyable and rewarding. Why should I have to give it up? I could have the best of both worlds, traditional medicine and alternative healing. This self-created bliss was the bliss of ignorance.

Several months before my 35th birthday, I had begun to feel a pattern of abdominal pain. The pain was sudden intense cramping that radiated to my back. Other symptoms were nausea, sweating, lightheadedness, and weakness. Within minutes the attack was full blown, lasting between twelve and twenty-four hours with equivalent intense pain. Somehow, I managed through my professional duties. Once finished, I had just enough energy to return home and go to bed. By the next morning the pain had completely subsided as if it never had happened.

In February, less than a month after my 35h birthday, the attacks were coming on a more frequent basis, about three weeks apart. By March, they were coming every two weeks, and I went to see a specialist in gastrointestinal disorders. He performed an extensive examination which included blood and urine study, X rays, and a fiber optic view of the inside of my upper small intestines and stomach. He diagnosed a chronic relapsing pancreatitis, which in my case had no cure. I knew from my medical training that the prognosis ranged from the attacks stopping suddenly for indefinite periods of time to fulminating pancreatitis with an 80% mortality rate. The ever-increasing progression of the attacks didn't look good. I began to probe deeply into my psyche for a psychological etiology that might manifest this disease process. I found nothing of significance and received no guidance from my inner teacher.

Five months after my birthday the attacks were coming every three days. I had recently given my first public lecture and discussed the dramatic healings that occurred in my work, but I could do nothing for myself. With my partners on vacation, my workload had increased significantly. I was up at 4:00 A.M. to meditate and to the hospital making rounds by 5:30, working until 10:00 or 11:00 and longer if there was an emergency. I loved it.

Then came the thirty minutes that were to alter my entire life.

I had finished my hospital rounds one Saturday morning and was working on some patient charts in my office when I felt an incredibly strong urge to meditate. After finishing the charts, I gave into the impress. I didn't understand what was happening as a vortex of energy with a magnitude I hadn't before experienced, reverberated through my body expanding my awareness into a superheightened state. Then a loud voice – not that of the inner teacher – said, "Your experience and training as an orthodox physician is completed. It's over." My "yes, but" machine came on: I talked about all my resistance, my patients, my partners, my family, my love of medicine. About a half hour later, the voice made it very clear that it didn't care. "You're going on a world journey that is to begin in a small place in Northern

Scotland and proceed through England, Egypt, India, Nepal near the Tibetan boarder, and perhaps to Japan, with a trip to China to come later. You will rekindle old soul memories and reshape childhood ideals about medicine to integrate alternative healing practices with traditional medicine." The last instruction the voice gave was to detach from everything.

Although my mind tried to rationalize this experience away, the deeper feeling resonating throughout my Beingness was to yield to the voice's greater truth rather than following with the pragmatic. The voice never came back, and I began to realize that within the human psyche, completely separate from the ego, existed autonomous forces beyond individuality. I followed the wisdom and truth that permeated the experience, and in six weeks everything was gone: practice, teaching positions, home, most of the furnishings, cars, and clothes.

Amazingly, I was now traveling to Findhorn, a place I had not even known about prior to the mediation. Now, I knew that Findhorn was a spiritual community in Northern Scotland. The people of Findhorn were warm, spiritually open and a diverse community. After becoming acquainted, I learned that I could teach people to feel body energy fields and to transfer healing energy into the body. Findhorn was my opening door to a wonderful odyssey of experience after experience that shifted and touched the essence of my being. Slowly, the whole quality, depth and character of my self-hood was changing, as exemplified by my journey into India.

My India journey required a whole sequence of shifts and transformations in my consciousness. As a snake molts its skin, my mode of travel through India was a metaphor for the many layers that were shed. I jetted into Bombay and took a turbo-prop up to Bangalore. My next destination was by train to Madras, and then I took a bus to Pondicherry. Later I rode a bicycle which I eventually placed on a wagon with hay, finally ending up walking. When I entered Oroville, I was in a rhythm that was almost diametrically opposed to the speed, intensity, and values of the West. I was in a extraordinary state of communion with India, a very familiar feeling, vibration, and knowing. Some part of me was so connected to the ambiance of India that the thought of staying resonated with a sense of harmony. It was in Oroville that I broke the spell of materialism because for just pennies a day I was in a sublime state of rapport and serenity with nature and the collective East-West community − my fantasy of living quietly and simply was germinating in the primordial soil of India.

Returning to the West was not in any of my immediate plans. Nevertheless, when I received the letter indicating my acceptance as a Fellow in the American College of Physicians, I decided to return for my final accolades in medicine. My mother's unexpected illness took me back to Southern California where I felt blessed to be at her side when she died. After my mother's death, I traveled to the vast expanse of Himalayas where I unleashed my deep pain and grief. I loved her deeply for all that she was and all she had given.

I returned to Southern California thinking I was gearing up to make my final move back to India. While in Los Angeles, I met the wife of the ex-ambassador to India at a Los Angeles Church of Religious Science function. She told me of a boy who lived in a village close to Bangalore and felt that a personal experience and meeting would be significant.

When I arrived back in India, I met the woman from Los Angeles, who had returned to India before me. Together we went to the boy's village, which was a virtual mud bath. As we walked on wooden planks over wet viscous soil and open sewage, I could see that all the construction was with adobe brick. Obviously, the people of this village and the boy were of a low caste in a country that to this day is still caste conscious.

We walked together to where they had set up a shrine between two huge ant hills. They had draped the enclosure between the ant hills with cloth and had placed flowers, fruit, incense and saffron throughout the inner court area. As we sat down, this old man began playing his rattle drum which created a rhythm as he beat the clacker on each side. Although the boy was in reality 20 years old and recently married, his behavior and demeanor were that of a 12 year old, and that is why I refer to him as a boy. In his childlike energy, he was quite immature, mundane and simple, but as the rhythm of the drums continued he suddenly began to change states of consciousness. He shifted into an intermediate state while putting his feet into these amazing shoes with sharp nails pointing straight up. He then began to stomp around on these shoes, and suddenly changing from speaking the local caste dialect to high Hindi, a formal and difficult language which was far beyond this boy's provincial ability.

In what took only an instant, his childlike demeanor and behavior were gone. Through the ritual energy of sound and those spectacular shoes, the boy shifted consciousness and was imbued with the ability, splendor and glory of a goddess energy. Radiating a glowing essence through the boy, the deity was now ready to answer questions. The enclosure filled with her magnificent presence erasing my rational doubt. With only one thought on my mind, I approached this boy – now goddess – with a ceremonial offering of a lime. I bowed and offered the lime. In high Hindi she responded by saying,

"Give me the $150.00 in your right pocket." No one knew about the $150.00 I had placed in my pocket prior to leaving for the village as an offering to the boy's caretakers. I laughed out loud, two thoughts quickly going through my mind: It's amazing how important money is here, and out of all possible responses, hers was the least anticipated. So I laughed again and said, "Yes, I want to give it to you." I handed the money over and said, " Well, I'm thinking about living in India." She looked at me and said, "Go home. Your destiny lies in the West."

India had stirred up an ancient memory that resonated throughout my being with a deep-felt bonding and connection, igniting a subsequent urge to reestablish the patterns behind the feeling of belonging and home. Although my affinity and kinship with India was important at some place within the psyche's being, it was painful to realize the truth of the obvious. Still, I quickly understood that my last few years of spiritual development and, indeed, my whole life moved toward a Western process with a compelling intensity. I decided to return home and telephoned my father to see if Sky Hi Ranch was available for lease, as a site for future conferences. At the core of being was a calling to broaden the approach to healing in the West with the vehicles of expanded states of consciousness and Unconditional Love.

Life is the great crucible for change and development. As events, experiences and circumstances manifest in one's life, it is important to yield to the inner forces calling for change. Spirit demands much and gives more.

Victoria's Story

The Rebirth of My Guides, My Angels

"It ain't so. It ain't so." I feel red hot as I slam the door to the backyard. Running to our secret hiding place, my hand pushes through the tall green grass with my squishy baby-faced doll trailing behind in my other hand. I mad at cousin Susie for what she say. I hate her. I hate her. I kill them...I kill them...I kick and rip her. Blonde hair and limbs lying around me, I kick one more time and then I cry and cry. My hands rubbing the tears away as they roll down my face. There. They dead now!

As you can see from this vignette, my early childhood was not easy. I never seemed to fit. My two younger brothers were more in harmony with my dad than I. I remember when he used to give them haircuts. I'd be waiting in line, and he'd say, "You can't have a haircut, you're a girl." I felt cheated because I wasn't a boy. On a hot day I would take off my tee-shirt like they did and get teased about it. The boys would gang up on me, but I still tried to play with them because there weren't any little girls to be my friend. Although I fondly remember my mother's love and support, more often than not she was emotionally distant and kept herself at arms length. So I felt alone.

I remember going into my closet and closing the door. Then I told my special friends how I wanted to go home and about my troubles, how hard it was living here. They would always say just the right things. We would build castles and then play in them. It was wonderful! Often we would agree to meet at certain places:

"Okay I'll meet you between Betty's and my garage to-morrow." They would be there; Sebastian, Aamoyaa, or one of the others. They were always there. They were my angels, my friends who understood and helped me with my troubles. When I was so upset about not getting a haircut from my dad, they told me that although I was not a boy, being a girl was special and would have many benefits too. I am not sure whether they were in my imagination or physically real. All I remember is that they were real to me and seemed very conscious of my life.

My cousin Susie was a practical little girl and seemed well adapted to living in this world, which I never did, or so I thought. Anyway, Susie said, "Victoria is a baby; she has baby friends." Although those words made me mad, I knew in my heart I had to give up my imaginary friends and get real. So my beloved doll with her big blue eyes was now in pieces and my friends were gone! I was between 4 and 5 years old, but I strongly felt I had a choice to stay in the world or go back my real home, to the other side. I decided to stay, but it killed me because I had to close down so much to remain here. My family really didn't understand me. They gave me only conditional acceptance and love – no one seemed there for me.

Shortly after I killed my doll and left my guides/friends, I began kindergarten suffering from a childhood depression that lasted for years. I don't remember ever really coming out of it until about age 15. I was very shy and gained a lot of weight. Without Aamoyaa, Sebastian and the others, I felt totally lost! My home life was troubled also. My mother was distant, and my dad was an alcoholic. At night he would come and tuck me in bed. I hated his alcoholic breath and his slobbering words: "you're my only daughter; I love you; you are beautiful." I didn't believe him. Now I suspect physical abuse, but I am not sure. Anyway, I am sure that it contributed to my depression and the blanked-out time in my life – I was very confused and didn't have much guidance.

When I was 15, I faced the realization that my life wasn't going to get better from the outside. I felt very self-conscious of my physical appearance; my weight, clothing and hair were all out of step with my peers. I felt like the cartoon character Baby Huey, diapers and all. As boys and girls began noticing each other and pairing up; I thought it could never happen for me. I had to change.

I decided to kill Baby Huey, the depressed, chubby, awkward little girl. At 15, strong and buoyant, I went on a massive diet. Today it would be called anorexia. I literally ate one Hostess cup cake a day. That was it. I lost tons of weight and probably looked like the walking dead. I felt like I was groping in the dark, but I changed my total image: weight, hair and clothes. It was a total change in my outer appearance.

After the big change, I asked my brother to say hi to this cute boy that I remember had sat next to me for a year in middle school. When he saw the new me for the first time he said, "who's that!" He had no clue. Suddenly, I was attractive, popular and dating. It was great. Yet I felt like I was putting on layers. This new image wasn't completely me. I felt as though I was acting.

Time went by and a number of years later I got married. Looking back on it, I felt that during my marriage I was out of touch with my spirituality and my guide/friends were just a vague memory. I was totally caught-up with my husband and the marriage. He was attending chiropractic college while I worked three jobs to keep him there. He didn't work a day in the five years we were married. I was totally committed to his education; his graduation was the central theme of our relationship . He let me call the shots. I needed the control.

About three years into marriage, the feelings associated with the Baby Huey image started to come back. I started putting on weight and was horrified. As time went by, I became more and more frustrated. I started having a fantasy about a man I had met, but it went nowhere. I was miserable, nothing was working right. I was distraught and contemplating suicide. I even experimented with closing all the windows and doors with the gas on. I wanted to see how it might feel – I chickened out but was still emotionally unbalanced. A few days later on a rainy night I was driving recklessly on a mountain road which had many hairpin curves. The car started into a spin straight over the edge of the cliff. In a flash I thought, *this is it.* Then, amazingly the car stopped just before going over. The car filled with a soft pink light that momentarily evaporated my fear and a soft voice permeated the whole car with two words: *Remember Love.*

In total awe, I sat in the car for several hours wondering if I was going crazy. Did it really happen? Still, I felt a sense of peace in my body, as if I had been showered with love. Nonetheless, I went straight home and looked in the phone book for a psychologist. Through the help I received, I was able to see the many flaws in our marriage and myself. Knowing that our marriage was not working for either of us, I decided to file for divorce.

Several years later, I met my second husband and we were blessed with our son, Drew. Although the marriage only lasted five and one-half years, Drew was the joy of my life. We have always been close with a bond of love that has truly enriched both of us. When he was five years old, I was in school working on a degree when one day I doubled over with extreme pain and cramping, and the next thing I remembered I was in a doctor's office with a IV in my arm and a gas mask over my face hearing someone say the ambulance was almost here. Unknown to me, I was dying from a grapefruit-size benign fibroid tumor that was entangled on the inside lining of my uterus. The tumor had been jarred and was hemorrhaging profusely.

All of a sudden, I'm walking through this golden white light that totally surrounds and engulfs me. I saw Sebastian and Aamoyaa walking toward me and I was filled with joy. Although I felt in pieces, my awareness streamed through all the separate parts of me, an instant awareness at many different levels. I locked arms with my two old friends and held them tight. It reminded me of the scene in the Wizard of Oz where Dorothy walks arm in arm with the scarecrow and lion. I am in Heaven I thought – this must be how it is.

I had perfect communication with my guides/friends, and was eager to bring them up to date on my life. I would think something and they would instantaneously know. Even though I was sure they already knew everything, they indulged me. They said, "Okay, well tell your story," and I just had to tell them. "Wait until you hear all this crazy stuff," I said. They listened, but I realized they didn't need to – they already knew. I remember thinking how perfect complete awareness was. To be fully known instantaneously: emotions, thoughts, beliefs, my entire being, it was just amazing.

As we walked arm in arm in this tunnel of light, I looked at the brilliant molecules that completely surrounded us. In what felt like an instant, I looked into a luminous particle knowing I could create an enchanted castle to live in. Every molecule was a new frontier, a new reality, a new creation waiting to happen. So many possible realities were overwhelming; besides, I had what I had craved and wanted – I was walking in being-to-being contact with long ago friends I loved.

I stopped looking at the light and concentrated on them as we walked up what seemed to be an elevated path, giving no thought to where we were going. I just felt happy and reassured in their arms that is – until I thought – Drew. I stopped in my tracks and said, "I have to go back."

Quickly, they turned to me and said, "But this is the day you were to depart. Is there a problem with that?"

With every fiber, every portion of my being I communicated, *my son!* I could feel it, taste it – as if with claws of total passion, I dug into the knowledge that I wanted to return to Drew. I knew my ex-husband would crush his spirit – without me, Drew simply would not survive.

They were gone and back in a flash: "We have been to the throne, and you have been granted an extension," they said with excitement. "If you agree, you'll be able to go back to life with your son in exchange for work we need done. Everything of necessity will be told to you, but for now all you need know is there are angels with skin who have forgotten who they are and need your help."

"Anything, anything, I want to go back to my son!"

Like two elegant dancers, they raised their arms in a full circle motion giving me the impression that they were cutting the energy of that moment. In an instant I was back – alive in the recovery room. Around me people stared with concerned expressions. I knew their thoughts as if I were still back with Sebastian and Aamoyaa. Intuitively, they knew something had happened to me, but they were only concerned with my physical well being, not with where I had been or with how my experiences had deepened my understanding of myself and life.

Nurses were coming and going as I faded in and out of consciousness. I saw beings of light in the room and in my mind I heard them talking. It was similar to when my car filled with pink light and I heard the words, *remember love.* The room appeared almost as radiant as the tunnel of light. A nurse came in and asked me about a blood transfusion. Simultaneously, I heard the nurse and an inner voice speaking.

"We need to give you a blood transfusion," said the nurse

"You don't need blood," from the inner voice

I said, "I don't need blood. I'm fine."

Then, I heard: "You will recover without needing blood. Drink a lot of water and take your algae tablets, which contain all the components you'll need for building blood."

I did recover quickly. I'd gone to the hospital on a Monday and was out by Friday, and five weeks later I was back on my feet and driving. Except for a few minor things, I have completely recovered and have enjoyed wonderful health.

For the next six months, I focused on my spiritual side; I read many spiritual books, began meditating regularly and spent a lot of time communing with nature. Still, I was confused; I was not the old Victoria. I was still connected to that other dimension. I was amazed at what I could see. People I knew began avoiding me because I would stare at them with big wide eyes. I loved to see their energy fields and the light coming off their bodies in different colors. My facial expressions must have been both revealing and alarming because I had a hard time disguising what I saw. The way I looked at them must have been frightening. Many times I saw what looked like newspaper smudge covering peoples eyes, ears or mouth, or coming out their throat. I began making associations to what I saw: no wonder so and so doesn't listen well. Some experiences scared me. One time, I was driving and looked in the rear view mirror. In the car behind me was a woman who had superimposed inside her the figure of an ape with fangs and a heavy matted fur coat. I slammed on the brakes and almost caused an accident. This woman was not the only one; what I saw within other individuals really upset me. Furthermore, energy streamed out my hands, affecting tape recorders, microwaves, televisions and video-recorders. It was all very traumatic and confusing. I began pleading with my guide/friends for help until mercifully these experiences began to dim down. Nonetheless, I remember being in a supermarket and hearing my guide say, "Get used to it; you're going to need to be in many common situations and receive information. Start to expand the use of your gift and become comfortable receiving on different levels."

Although I am evolving and growing each day, it has taken time to become comfortable with my gift. I left teaching not too long after a guide suggested that owning a business utilizing my gifts was on the horizon. I remember complaining, "I can't start a business; I wouldn't have medical insurance or a retirement program."

The angels just giggled and said, "Are you planning to get sick?"

I said, no.

"Then why do you need insurance," they asked.

My teaching job, insurance, and pension plan are all gone. I followed my heart and opened the Angel Connection. Although I have a part-time bookkeeping job, my passion continues to be my business. The work I do is directly connected to spirit. As a self-employed consultant and healer, I use my guides and angles with aroma therapy, crystal healing and channeling to assist people in need. My desire is to be of service to others while all the time remembering that my top priority is my dear son, Drew. I will always know that it was my deep love for him that brought me back.

Lee Coit

Does Life Really Make Sense?

In the mid 1970's, I was feeling very unsure about the direction of my life. The question "Does life really make sense" reverberated through my mind with no clear-cut answer. Certainly, my life didn't feel rational or sane. I had just gone through a painful divorce, and my ex-business partner and I were engaged in a heated dispute about our business. At the same time, people I trusted were taking advantage of me in other business investments. I felt angry, misused, and very much alone. If there was a God out there, He must be having a great time tormenting me; He certainly wasn't loving and caring. Besides, I had tried to live a good life and felt I deserved better. I began questioning everything.

Within this growing sense of desperation, I longed for practical answers. I didn't want classes, churches, or philosophies. I really needed to experience something personal, to touch what most people called "God". I felt that if the universe was based on divine principles, then I wanted to experience those principles. Still, my many experiences with life's betrayals had made me quite skeptical.

One day I realized that my successful achievements had come from hard work and dedication. I had no outstanding abilities to make life easy, nor was I brilliant, a good athlete or particularly handsome. I had learned that, if I wanted to accomplish something, I had to devote myself to it. This is how I had become successful in the business world.

Using the same formula, I came up with a plan, to try to discover these governing universal principles. I decided to dedicate one year of my life questing for the truth, which I hoped would bring a sense of peace, joy and renewed value to my life. I had only one requirement: I wanted these principles to contact me directly and not to be interpreted by anyone else.

My plan was to dedicate every day to the search. As a way of tackling my weight problem, I began each day's exploration by running 2 ½ miles to the beach. Wanting a personal contact with the Divine, I strolled near the ocean and sat in contemplation on the rocks. I waited. This was going to be between me and God, if there was such a phenomenon. I felt that if I gave God a year to show up, and He didn't, then either He wasn't there or He didn't care. I was prepared for a "no show" as the probable outcome. I felt the whole project would probably just fizzle like a cheap firecracker. Still, I wanted to give this quest my full effort because I wanted to feel at peace in knowing I had done the best I could no matter what the outcome.

Every day I ran to beach, walked near the ocean and waited. Little by little, things began to happen. At first, these occurrences seemed small and incomplete, but they brought me a good feeling about pressing forward. I remember waking up one night out of a deep sleep and feeling restless. Turning on the TV, I listened to a television preacher, whose emotion-packed cadence went on and on until I almost fell back asleep; then something he said about total commitment struck me as important and I thought about it as he rambled on. The next day I had an experience that reinforced the message I had felt so relevant the night before. This was followed by a series of unrelated coincidences about commitment. Even in the simplest of form, the truth and insight that they revealed was exactly what I wanted.

I went from being almost a total skeptic to a doubting-experimenter. For instance, I decided that reading the Bible before I ran to the beach might help in my quest to find God, so at random, I would open the Bible and read a couple of paragraphs, then let what I read percolate through my mind as I ran to the beach. During the day, the part of myself that was distrustful watched for coincidences that would relate to the stories I had read in the Bible. I found myself looking for the times when they didn't work, for if the principles governed the universe, they should work in all instances and be easy to find; once I was aware them.

One morning I opened to a chapter in the Bible that goes on and on enumerating who begat who. Well, I thought, *I really have proof now*. This can't possibly have anything to do with universal principles or my life. When I read further, the quotation chastised the Hebrew people as a stiff-necked, stubborn generation. As I ran that morning, I thought about the reasons why God was displeased with Moses' people: they built golden calves; they disobeyed him; and with every tribulation they argued with Him. As I ran along with all these negative thoughts racing through my mind, I realized I had a stiff neck. I laughed out loud. After all the wonderful happenings in my life, I still doubted there was a God or Divine principles. I was a stiff-necked person too! As my laughter subsided, I noticed my neck was pain free. Wow!

I now began to add to my original experiment by applying the creative process that I had used in my business. Whenever I had a problem with a new advertising campaign, I would just let the problem percolate in the back of my mind as I went about my daily activities. All of a sudden, like a light bulb going on, the answer would just pop into my head. If that's the way I created a successful advertising agency, why not use the same intuition to solve my everyday problems. After that I began letting my questions simmer in the back of my mind. Without forewarning, I would suddenly receive answers that helped me or sent me in the right direction. After a year, one of the directions I received was to go to Europe for an extended period of time.

I decided to continue my experiments in Europe and invited Lynn, my girlfriend, to go with me. Before we left, she wanted to say goodbye to her family in San Francisco.

About the same time, I read a wonderful book on Christianity, which stated as part of its message this idea: in the truest sense, only one guy ever totally tried Christianity. I decided to be the second guy. Thus, when I had an action or a decision that needed to be made, I would literally ask myself "what would Jesus do?" This meshed nicely with the creative listening I was doing.

Before going to San Francisco, Lynn told me that her stepfather Hal had been a big problem in her life. When we arrived for our visit, I found he was as bad as she had said: a rough character who made it clear that he thought that the world was totally crazy. I asked what would Jesus do about Hal and the answer I received was "Let him be." I remembered thinking that Jesus didn't go around forcing people to follow him, and the phrase forgive 70 X 7 kept coming to me. So, I just decided to keep treating him as if nothing was wrong.

That evening we decided to go out to dinner, and I asked Hal if he would like to come. In a gruff voice he replied, "No, those darn restaurants just rip you off. They charge twice as much as the food is worth; the service is no good, and the food is usually cold."

"Fine!" I said. As we were about to leave, I remembered 70 X 7 and asked again, "Are you sure you don't want to come?"

"Well," he said, "I can see that I'm not going to get anything to eat around here."

At dinner I asked what he did for a living? He told me that he was a crane operator whose job it was to delicately place and position things that were often awkward to handle. Because of his skill level, he was called in for the most dangerous and complicated jobs, like his current job, the laying of a large pipeline.

I said, "That must be a very rewarding job."

"Naw, its a junky job."

I said, "What would you like to do?"

His whole demeanor seemed to transform as his eyes lit up with wonder. He told me that his dream was to make it as a trombone player. Apparently, he had been a talented musician in a little band during the Depression, but because of the economic hardship of the time, he was forced into his current occupation out of sheer desperation. I don't recall saying anything extraordinary during , but I had listened with heartfelt empathy. I thought how frustrating and bitter it must have been to let go of something you love, knowing you could never go back to it.

The next morning Hal decided not to go to work, so we could continue talking. As our conversation progressed, I shared many of my personal sorrows and frustrations; how life often didn't seem fair to me. I revealed my own pain in an honest way, telling him that I believed that there was a purpose to all our experiences. Later, after Hal went to work, his wife said, "You know, Hal and I have been in the process of getting a divorce, but last night he said, 'maybe we should give it another chance.' I don't know what you've done to him, but he was a changed man this morning."

Lynn spoke up and said, "Lee's doing this experiment, asking 'what Jesus would do' in different circumstances. He has been directed to some books that have helped him understand his personal search for universal principles and truth."

"Could you find a book for me?" asked Lynn's Mother.

The pied piper of books was not the way I saw myself, but Lynn's mother was determined that I would be able to find her just the right book. So, when we went to lunch in Tiberon, I picked out a book for her and another for me. Unbeknown to me, her insistences led to a series of events which took my self-imposed experiment to a level beyond my wildest dreams.

On a table next to the cash register was the book, *Love is Letting Go of Fear,* by Jerry Jampolski. When I started to peruse through it, I knew right away I had found a jewel in a sea of ink and paper. Although the pictures seemed silly and the text was a bit childlike, the truth contained within it engendered a feeling of love towards its simple but profound message. I bought and read it that very day.

When the book mentioned *A Course in Miracles,* I envisioned a cult of people in white robes dancing around candles worshipping a Guru and acting spiritual, which was the direct opposite of truth that I was seeking. I drove back to the bookstore and asked to see the *Course in Miracles.*

The sales clerk said, "We're all out."

"Well that's okay, I really didn't feel any connection with it."

"Well, if you want them, they are published right here in Tiburon." After she gave me the directions to the publisher, I inquired about Jerry Jampolski's office, knowing it was in Tiburon too.

She giggled, "It's right behind this bookstore." This was the way my life was going. If I was to do something, it always was right in front of me.

The door to Jampolski's office was locked, but I noticed a sign on another door, which read "Attitudinal Healing Center." When I went in to inquire about his office hours, the lady who greeted me said Jampolski was directly involved in the center and explained how they were treating children with terminal diseases. They had a tour in an hour, and I was definitely intrigued enough to wait for it.

I went outside and stood on the wharf adjacent to the building and looked across the Bay at San Francisco. Someone behind me said, "You've come this far. What are you afraid of?" I immediately looked around, but there was nobody there. Because the voice was loud, I looked under the landing pier thinking someone might be docking their boat. No one was there! The voice was certainly not in my head. Previously, my inner listening had been in the form of thoughts that would pop into my head when I was working on a problem or, at times, a dialog with what seemed to be an inner presence, but this was a specific audible voice.

In hindsight, I am amazed at my immediate reaction. I was angry! My mind began spinning: *I am not afraid to go down there and get those damn books, if that's what I'm supposed to do. I'm not afraid – it doesn't mean I have to like them.*

As I drove toward the address the saleslady had given me, a mental picture of robes, candles and Gurus kept running through my mind. I thought: if these people try to sign me up or try to make me join something, I'm out of there.

Arriving, I knocked on the door and a man in tennis clothes answered and said impatiently, "What do you want?"

I said, " I understand this is where the *Course in Miracles* are published and I want to look at it."

"I am late for a tennis match. I don't have time for you to look at them. Do you want to buy them or don't you?"

I said, "I'm not going buy them unless I can see them." Reaching behind on a table, he handed me a brown wrapped package. As I held the heavy package in my hands I asked, "How much are they?". He said, "29 dollars." I never saw the book's cover until after I had paid for them, deciding it was a good deal because I had been spending ten dollars for smaller books. I bought the books on weight alone.

There were two large and one small book in the package: the text, a workbook and a teacher's manual. Wanting to keep things simple and easy, I grabbed the smaller teacher's manual. Before finishing the first page, I realized this was the next step. I felt as if these books had been written for me. I had no trouble understanding them and was eager to start. The workbook had daily lessons designed for a one-year period; I thought.... Wow... I'll do this as I travel in Europe.

The course states over and over that its purpose is to prepare you to listen to your inner voice, to substitute the mind's chatter and conditioning for inner guidance in solving problems. This is exactly what I did for the next seven months in Europe. I followed each lesson in a disciplined manner just as it was prescribed, slowly perfecting my inner listening while gleaning a new perception of life. My car became my meditation chamber. If the lesson for the day was to be done every 15 minutes, I did just that. As I studied the daily lessons, things happened that made the exercises relevant to what I was experiencing as I traveled around Europe. It was marvelous. I began using my inner guidance for all decisions. I used it as a map; for exchanging money; finding places to sleep or camp, for everything. I made no significant decisions with my mind.

Once as we were driving near Edinburgh, Lynn was frustrated and angry, trying to use a tangled-up map to guide us out of the city. I remember grabbing the map and throwing it into back seat . "Don't worry about it," I said, then by following my inner guide's directions I drove straight to the freeway. This incident was probably the straw that broke the camel's back. After about a month, Lynn couldn't take the intensity of my total shift from relying on intellect to that of inner guidance. She returned home, and I continued asking, "Left, right or straight ahead" at every crossroads and intersection. Using my inner resource, I found my way throughout the rest of my trip.

There are so many reasons for using inner guidance instead of one's own mind. Today, I don't even think about using my mind, unless it's for something simple like taking out the garbage. Looking at life from the big picture, I realize I often don't know what my real choices are. When Lynn flew home, she left me an extra sleeping bag and all the gear we had used for camping. Considering there was enough equipment and supplies for two, I envisioned a lovely lady as my companion for the rest of my European trip and, as my fantasy grew, even a life partner.

Although I had no formal plans to meet with my daughter in Europe, I had the casual thought, if I have an opportunity to see her that would be good. Through my inner listening, I felt guided to visit her. Therefore, I drove to Montpellier in Southern France where she had been staying only to find that she had moved. I copied her phone number from my notebook onto a piece of paper. I called her several times with no answer. Frustrated at the difficulty in determining the right coins for the European pay phones, I finally gave up and decided to leave.

On my way out of town, I saw a pay phone and stopped to give it one more chance. Instead of reaching in my pocket for the number I had written down, I reached for my notebook. That's when I discovered I had transposed two digits and had been dialing the wrong number. When I called the right number a man answered and said he expected Elese to call from Paris in a few minutes. He would have her call me at the pay phone. When she called she said, "I want to talk to you. I want to see you," so, I stayed the night to have lunch with her the next day.

During lunch, I found out that my daughter was very upset. We talked for a long time, which seemed to raise her spirits, but I was still very concerned. As we walked out to my car she said, "What's all that stuff in you car?"

I told her about Lynn: the two sleeping bags, two chairs and all the gear. She laughed and said, "I'm not doing anything for the next 30 days; why don't I go with you?"

For the next month, my daughter and I had a wonderful reunion, which gave her plenty of time to express her feelings and thoughts. I shared my feelings about my divorce from her mother. It was a healing time for both of us, a time to grow closer. Besides, we had endless fun together.

After Lynn left, I was feeling lonely, but now I was enjoying many beautiful scenic campgrounds with my lovely daughter. At night around the camp fire, we'd have sing-alongs with the many boys she seemed to attract. Once, we stayed up so late singing that we were politely asked to go to sleep. It was a wonderful time of laughter and joy with plenty of good people.

When Elese had asked to join me, I remember my immediate thought had been: this is going to make it difficult for me to meet anybody with my daughter along. At the time, that was my agenda. I am so happy I abandoned my plan, for it all turned out perfect. When finally our time was up, I put her on the train back to Paris.

As I was walking out of the station I heard a voice say, "Now, which would you choose?" My mind's agenda would never have brought me any experience greater than the father-daughter healing and joy I experienced during those glorious 30 days. It confirmed my mind's lack of ability to know the true nature of my own needs.

After returning from Europe, I continued to explore the *Course in Miracles*. More and more I relied on my inner guidance/teacher, which lead me to write the book *Listening* that is now published by Hay House. Without the chatter of the mind and the conditioning of the personality, life is a miracle. The only question is, can we listen?

Yes, we can!

Judith-Annette Milburn, Ph.D.

"I will never leave you or forsake you. I never have and I never will." From the moment I heard these words in a Jean Houston workshop, I knew their truth was central to my life's journey. Through my many life experiences and changes their spirit-filled meaning has always guided me with comfort, caring, and strength. Regardless of what appears to be happening, I now know I have been cared for all of my life – I need not worry. When I was growing up, I would never have consciously anticipated the far-reaching life theme reflected in these words or imagined myself as I am today.

I grew up in Lubbock, a growing town on the western plains of Texas. It was a very safe environment with lots of open space and plenty of freedom within the perspective, organization and structure of a strong Christian and predominantly Southern Baptist community. My family was very active in the church, public schools and the community, and I remember my grandfather being called "the judge" because his wisdom was helpful in mediating disputes.

From my earliest memories, I was fully involved with my family in the church, which provided me with many opportunities to grow and mature through its worship services and church activities. My life's context was incorporated within Sunday school, Bible studies, devotionals, prayer meetings with my father and playing the piano. Committed to becoming a missionary, I became deeply grounded in my faith and love of this great spiritual tradition; its teachings touched the core of my being. Within the chalice of the church's spiritual perspective, community, and warmth, I developed as a person. Its support and order provided me a time of enrichment, value and growth, and although my knowledge was limited to the Christian room as taught by Southern Baptists, I was very much within God's mansion.

I was very headstrong as a young child, a "ring-tail tutor," as my aunt would say. When we would return home from an outing, she often said that before she was in the front door I would be dashing out the back kitchen door running through the vacant lot behind our house. At three years old, my mother brought my baby brother home from the hospital . I vaguely remember acting up, but God knows what I was doing. Still, given the fact that my sister was two years younger and with the arrival of my brother, I was probably feeling displaced and seeking attention. While still recuperating in her bed, my Mother said, "Come here so I can spank you." My anxious, yet defiant eyes immediately locked on to my Mother as I backed up against her dresser. With a confidence beyond my years I said, "Be ye kind." Although I am sure I was strongly admonished, I don't remember receiving a spanking, but to this day I can remember and recite the full Sunday school verse: "Be ye kind and tender hearted forgiving one another."

This experience with my mother was my earliest memory of a knowing, a power and a presence beyond my inherent capabilities. As I look back on that experience and the many that would follow, I am aware of a transcendent quality that engenders a feeling of design or pattern which passes through my life.

This Divine thread of guidance is easily seen as I reflect back on my life's journey. In fact, seen as a metaphor, my first day of school reveals this lifelong pattern. My school was four or five blocks away from our house, and on that first day, I was to return home for lunch. I knew the way back home, but I became confused when I exited the main school door, and instead of going around the block towards my home, I went the other way. I walked for quite a while and finally ended up in downtown Lubbock near our church, the First Baptist Church. From there, I knew my way home.

This sanctuary was symbolic of my spiritual home, where the essence of my spiritual being was nurtured and grounded in Christian values. Finding my way to my true spiritual essence has always been my life's journey. It has not been an easy or a direct route but, as within a maze, my life has flowed through many turns, dead ends, and course corrections with an ever constant urge to manifest and evolve towards my own spiritual alter and Divine awareness.

As a child and through my adolescence, my strong will and rambunctious character were tempered by two very strong forces. First, my father's word was not to be disputed, nor his authority challenged. Although he was a kind and good natured man, he was in charge and not to be contested. I grew into a courteous, respectful and kind young lady and knew how to fit and function appropriately within my family and church's values and perspective. Secondly, my earliest talking memory was of the next-door neighbor lady telling me not to stutter. As a little girl and all the way through high school, I had a difficult time speaking. The stuttering was most pronounced when I first started to say something and eased as I became more relaxed. I could hardly say my own name because the "J" sound was so difficult. This was extremely disconcerting and caused me feelings of inadequacy.

Despite my feelings of embarrassment, I was sometimes moved into action beyond my poor self-image. For instance, the other junior high schools in town had a "Morning Watch Program," and I felt our school deserved such a program too. Having a friendly and comfortable relationship with our principle made requesting the program easier. He put me in charge, and I coordinated the 20-minute program every morning before class. I arranged for our speakers, introduced them, and played the piano for the devotional singing. I'm not totally sure how I accomplished all this without being totally humiliated, for my stuttering was still a major problem. Certainly, I drew strength from something bigger and beyond myself.

From childhood through high school, I participated in the Sunday night program at our Baptist church. In this teaching program, we all participated in the lessons, and thus, I was encouraged and supported to speak in front of an audience. Out of this program came the opportunity to give 10-15 minute devotionals to other gatherings, including adult groups. In spite of my stuttering, my devotional talks were well received, so much so that I was invited back many times.

During this period in my life, I was absorbed into the Baptist theology and community. For the most part, I accepted and was comfortable with my Baptist faith and never dramatically challenged its authority. Even during my early years in college, I was very much committed and saw myself as a future missionary.

Then, I met my future husband, who did not share my ideals of becoming a missionary and whose religious beliefs differed from those of my family and religious community. Although he was raised in a Baptist family, he was not involved in the church and only attended Sunday services on occasion with me. Much more worldly than my family, he occasionally drank alcohol and enjoyed dancing, which I had never been allowed to do while living at home. These differences made my parents unhappy with my decision to get married, and I didn't know until the day of my wedding if my father would even walk me down the aisle. Even though I knew I was going against my family, tradition, teachings and community, I felt compiled to follow this strong urge to move in this new direction. In hindsight, breaking this taboo by leaving the family nest was a necessary step for my future development and growth.

A directing Force, beyond my conscious knowledge and personal control, is the guiding energy behind the thread that weaves its way through my life. It helped me to shift directions, gain new experiences, step out of my family environment, and learn to take care of myself through my many experiences in married life. The marriage challenged my entire upbringing, and now, it took me to the edge of an absolute taboo, divorce. Here again, I was pushing the family's limits, for in my world, divorce was only for movie stars in California, not nice girls from Texas. Since my family had opposed the marriage, I was hoping the divorce would be lesser of two evils. Still, I didn't know if life even existed after a divorce. Like with my marriage, I was now exploring unknown territory.

Three years after the divorce I enrolled in graduate school at the University of Maryland and immersed myself in my doctoral studies as my life's thread began to stitch into a new direction. Because I had never considered attending graduate school, the opportunity to move across country and begin my advanced studies was exciting. With this opportunity, I was again exploring – like in childhood, I was rushing out the back door into an open expanse. Likewise, I extended my boundaries by attending an ecumenical spiritual group. The people were warm, kind, and beautiful, and the Sunday service with its non-traditional liturgy was inspirational. I went often.

After graduate school, I remarried and moved to California. My second husband and I joined the Unitarian church, which expanded my growing spiritual diversity and social development. I learned to enjoy dancing and to be less judgmental about social drinking, even though I still drank sparingly. I became comfortable with my femininity and body, which allowed for my greater appreciation of my sexuality. Now, I was engaging life with an openness that would carry me into experiences and realms that I would never have dreamed existed, especially from within the context of my childhood experiences.

In the late 70's, two significant events happened that began a process of shifting the very nature and perspective of my being and life. Both experiences had the sublime otherworldly energy of my "Be ye kind" childhood experience, and the *feeling and force* behind my determination to move forward with what I had to do: marriages, divorce, graduate school, and new spiritual directions. The first experience happened at the Humanistic Psychology Conference held in Toronto where Jean Houston gave her presidential address for the Humanistic Psychology Association. I sat in the upper balcony watching and listening to her powerful and moving speech. At some point, a feeling and sense of a "long finger" stretched down through the air, pointing directly at her, accompanied by the words "There, you will study with her." I can still feel the experience of my entire being opening to her presence. I was deeply moved.

Not long after my experience with Jean Houston, I attended a conference sponsored by the Center of Integral Medicine. Again, the "long finger" stretched down accompanied by the words, "You will go to Egypt with him" as Brugh Joy, M.D., spoke about his experience inside the Great Pyramid of Cheops, and his transformation from his medical practice into teaching expanded states of consciousness. With these numinous declarations, I knew my path would include these two significant spiritual teachers, as my life's spiritual thread was now visibly weaving itself into my world.

Three years later, after a devastating divorce from my second husband, I went to my first Jean Houston conference. At the workshop, I had several profound experiences resulting in an opening of my conscious awareness. On the last night, I had a power happening that clearly surpassed the others. I had gone to bed filled with a sense of harmony, serenity and peace, feeling like I was moving in the right direction. In the morning, I woke up out of a dream with a sublime feeling of trust. There was something more going on in my mind other than the everyday chatter I was used to hearing. Another voice was now available –similar to the voice that accompanied the "long finger" experiences. I was told I could trust what I heard. Through careful and conscious listening, I was now attending to what I identified as my intuitive voice. In time, it became easier to recognize as my confidence grew from the guidance I received.

Six weeks later I was at U.C.L.A. attending a conference of the American Humanistic Psychology Association. A friend told me of a sub-group who were exploring altered states of consciousness. Regardless of the possible rules and even though I was not a member, I was moved by inner listening to follow this strong transpersonal "urge-knowing" to attend their meeting. In hindsight, I doubt they could have resisted this force which was pressing me into action as it had in the past. I was learning to consciously follow it!

I arrived early and joined others around a large recreational table made of heavy wood. When the lights were dimmed, they told us to quiet our minds and open to the unseen. I was awed by the profound shifts and experiences in altered awareness, with a few participants channeling information. Suddenly, out of nowhere, a woman sitting directly across from me said, "There is someone on the other side of the table with heavy energy." I didn't know what "heavy energy" was, but I knew she was talking about me, so I said,

"It's me." My pronouncement started a series of interactions that profoundly altered and transformed my entire being. Although to this day, I'm not completely sure what happened, I do know that I followed her instructions to focus my attention on her third eye chakra, while at same time consciously attuning to my own 6th chakra, located slightly above the eyebrows in the center of my forehead. I remember her asking people who worked with healing energy to gather around me using loving energy to clear my field. I felt this incredible opening through my body and energy system as what felt like divine love poured into my entire being. The day after this experience, I knew something had altered my very experience of reality and that I needed to be tender and easy with myself. This profound awakening resonated throughout my being for the next several days, and indeed, has never left me.

This experience opened me to a new level and vaster experience of being in the world, taking me deeper into myself. The spiritual reality behind the "long finger" and the "Be ye kind" childhood experience was now an ever present part of my existence. These transcendent experiences were no longer just being done to me, but were a quality of spirit within me, whose presence I was beginning to explore consciously. This was my initiation into this spiritual dimension that always has been active in my life and all life, as I see it now. I saw myself like the potter's clay, willing to be an open vessel through which this sublime relationship could express itself.

Now, it was my time to work with the appointed teachers.

The "young, dumb and full of gum" part of myself began the arduous task of clearing, harmonizing, awakening and transforming self through the guidance and light of two extraordinary teachers. It has not always been easy or comfortable, yet their radiance, warmth and love has led to many mysterious and enlightening experiences which have brought a quality to my life that is priceless. Two special memories move me to this very day: The wonder of experiencing unconditional love as energy at the Heart Initiation Conference with Brugh and the awe of being reconnected with personal feelings of the ancient wisdom of China with Jean. This ongoing process of deepening and unifying these multidimensional aspects of my self has led to a remarkable range, depth, and variety of experiences, with numerous realizations and revelations. Many have inspired me while others have been painful and humbling.

I recall how excited I was to be going to Egypt with Brugh Joy, as had been prophesied many years earlier. As I climbed Mount Sinai on my camel's back, the sun rose up over the mountain, illuminating this glorious morning desert and the valley below. I remember imagining what the experiences of Moses and the Children of Israel must have been like, as if I were reliving them. As we rode up the mount, I heard a voice say, "I, the Lord God am one God and I have many names." Although the voice spoke as the masculine Jehovah, which was consistent with my childhood experience of God, I now understood it differently. It was clear to me that this 'God' was speaking as a Divine Spirit, an inner spiritual experience and quality. The "many names" referred to the many forms in which the Transcendent expresses Itself, and gender was not an issue. This experience of God/the Transcendent filled my heart, my entire being with ecstasy and joy while greatly expanding my earlier concepts.

On the same trip during the time set aside for "dream work," I shared a dream with our group which I felt announced what a wonderful spiritual person I was. In the dream, I'm in the living room of a house I had owned. Three of the walls were completely covered by full-length mirrors. A man from a prior relationship and I were sitting in meditation. We were fully connected energetically and exploring sublime spiritual realms. Expecting praise at the end of my dream narration, I was a little surprised when Brugh asked me to describe the man. I ran off about a half dozen adjectives like arrogant, self-centered, prideful and manipulative, all the time waving my pointed finger as if I was chastising the man right in front of the group. At that point, Brugh said that because the room was mirrored the soul was informing me about myself; the fact that I was wagging my finger in the present only amplified my lack of awareness.

I was totally unconscious to this part of myself and would have never claimed those characteristics unless my soul had symbolized my plight with this dream communication. It was like an ice pick had shattered a carefully guarded self-image. To this day I can remember my feelings of humiliation; I thought surely Brugh would never want to work with me again.

Floating down the Nile River, I learned that my journey of awakening, my journey towards wholeness included integrating of all aspects of self, whether my ego liked it or not! After some reflection, I knew that bringing this dream forward meant I was ready to really learn the nonjudgmental perspective of the heart center. To travel this path, I realized I must be willing to exercise this greater level of honesty, if my work with any teacher was to flourish.

Through the portal of Unconditional Love, I was ready to utilize non-judgment in observing my shadow, the disowned parts of myself. Without this shift in consciousness from self-judgment to unconditional love, I would have been merely rehashing attempts to prove I was good enough, blocking my deeper exploration. As I settled down, I realized that the escaping rush of hot air that had left me deflated meant that there were probably many more dark dirigibles floating around in my psyche. Through this dream, my soul had initiated my shadow work.

As a psychologist, I continued to be of service to others at the Center for Conscious Living, which I founded in 1985. Working with others has helped me to deepen my appreciation for how the soul works through the experiences of the ego, the "I" part of the psyche. Together they weave in and out creating a magnificent tapestry of life, deepening our relationship with the transcendent. I am currently writing a book to help individuals experiencing a "personality-spiritual" collapse or expansion – where one's life doesn't work in the same way as it once did. These gifts of transformation and development require a mature examination and approach to all aspects of psyche, such as the shadow and wounded child and all belief systems. This painful-joyful journey ushers in expanded experiences of selfhood, Life, and the Transcendent which sustains all.

My understanding of the essence of, "I will never leave you or forsake you: I never have and I never will," grows with my appreciation for how Spirit works in the unfolding of my life. I have gratitude for the promise imbedded these words, regardless to what appears to be happening or my fear of what might take place. Even though I don't understand how it works, it is the core of my reality and the basis for my faith. These words engender a courage to open to more of who I am and to take the next step and the next. I trust the process of my unfolding.

Paula Shaw

The EST in My Life (Erhard Seminars Training)

"You're all assholes; your life doesn't work because you're all assholes; you don't know your ass from a hole in the ground; you're all righteous assholes."

These were the first words out of our trainer's mouth, and over the course of the training, I delighted in discovering just how much of an asshole I really was!

Back in 1975, I was an out of work actress with plenty of problems. Like so many people, I had numerous emotional issues that kept recurring. I had trouble with my relationships, and my dream of being an actress was falling by the wayside. I felt depressed, angry and frustrated; a sense of despair and hopelessness permeated my life. Over the years I had been in and out of short term therapy with an attitude of "fix the pain now." Later, I realized that my core belief was that nothing worked for me, which sabotaged all my efforts. At the time I was really hurting and in a lot of pain.

I had heard about this thing called EST. A number people had told me it was a powerful experience. I called a few trusted friends who had taken the training and they all said, "GO!" Still I was afraid to have high expectations because I didn't want them to be dashed – nothing worked for me. At the time the training cost several hundred dollars, which was a lot of money to invest in myself and therefore, a real effort. Nonetheless, I registered in my last-minute style the day before the training; because at the time they were training two groups concurrently, they just happened to have an opening.

Throughout the first day and a half, people went wild over the 13 agreements that each individual had to commit to uphold before being able to take the training. They were relatively simple items. The ones I remember were: be on time for each training session; don't eat or drink during the training; complete the entire training; don't bring any watches or timepieces into the training room; no alcohol or drugs during the entire length of the training; no leaving the training area except at designated breaks; no talking during the training. One example of the many challenges the trainer had to deal with was:

The trainer said, "You all agreed not to bring a time piece into the room. Those that have a time piece please raise your hands."

The woman next to me raised her hand and said, "I have one, but it's in my purse."

Trainer: "You agreed not to bring a timepiece into the room. It's in your purse, which is in the room, so you broke your agreement. Please take it to the back of the room and check it in at the desk."

I was simply amazed at how everyone reacted. Nearly every agreement was challenged at least once with many challenged over and over again. People screamed, yelled, and fought with the trainer. They tried every way they could to pull it apart. I sat there and listened as the trainer skillfully pointed out our lack of integrity because we had given our word to keep our commitments.

The whole process would have been funny, except I realized that the only difference between me and any of the trainees who challenged a particular agreement was that any objections, justifications and rationalizations I had were revealed to me as lies by the process of the trainer working with each person. On and on the challenges went, and one after another they were met by the trainer with the fact that we were very reasonable people who were so stuck in our righteousness we couldn't see the forest for the trees. Then, I realized the truth of what the trainer was pointing out, that our lives didn't work because we didn't keep our agreements. *You are your word.*

The trainer told us about the mouse and the maze: a mouse was put into a maze with four tunnels. At the end of one of the tunnels was some cheese, and the mouse soon learned to run down that tunnel to get the cheese. When the cheese was no longer placed at the end of that tunnel, the mouse continued to run down that tunnel for a number of trials; however, since there was no longer anything there, the mouse eventually stopped going down that tunnel. In contrast, human beings who have found cheese once will forever run down a tunnel with no cheese because to be right is equivalent to survival.

The mind is like a movie. The past is represented by the exposed film with the present and the future represented by undeveloped film. Everything that has ever happened to us is recorded as though it is exposed on film. This includes everything: thoughts, feelings, behaviors, events, successes and failures.

The mind is like a reference librarian, always checking into past picture frames to make sure we will survive in our current situation. This is done swiftly and unconsciously for most people. In all situations, the vigilant mind quickly issues orders to either proceed or stop by referencing our past to determine if we're able to survive in our present circumstances.

Since the mind is concerned with its survival, in many situations the images it references can be totally to our detriment. One of the many examples in my life where the mind's concern for survival was of no benefit to me was when I was struggling to find work as an actress. I felt guilty and dependent on my mother because she sent me some money every few months. Not only was I ungrateful for my mother's support but ironically I blamed her for sending me the money because I thought it lessened my motivation to find acting work. I reacted by getting lesser jobs because I knew that I could count on my mother's money. The pictures and beliefs in my mind made taking her money evidence of my inability, dependence, and moral ineptitude. My mind had referenced an image of how I could be okay (survival) by taking her money while at the same time furnishing an image of being dependent, unable and guilty. This image forced me to struggle with a confused and false sense of integrity. Therefore, I had no choice or responsibility in accepting her money because my reaction was "the effect" of the image created by my mind. As long as I stayed unconscious to my mind's survival game, I would be stuck in this detrimental pattern which would continue to repeat endlessly.

When through EST I became conscious of how the mind works, I was able to turn around the whole situation by choosing and taking responsibility. When I chose to be grateful for my mother's loving support, I was taking responsibility and choosing my response. This subsequently changed all my actions regarding my chosen profession. I said to myself: I am lucky to have a mother who is willing to encourage my desire to be an actress. I saw it as a gift of love rather than a confirmation of an image of old thought patterns that my mind had dug up to allow it to survive. When I totally accepted the money as support, my life changed and I began to get work.

For the most part human beings live very reasonable lives. They often see themselves as the effect or the victim of circumstances in their lives. They don't explore their feelings, thoughts and points of view. Certainly, I was very reasonable in accepting the image of being unable, dependent and guilty. I was an adult still taking money from my mother. Nevertheless, that very reasonable belief was killing my chances as an actress. When I saw myself as the "source" of life, I could then choose to take responsibility for my life. Sadly, most people are reasonable; they see their life as a consequence or effect of some other source: "I can't get another job because I have to be sure I can pay the bills and support my family." "I can't be an actress because I am not that good" "I can't ask that woman out to dinner because she's too attractive." Sounds *reasonable* to me! Sounds like your mind is *right* again, and since most people believe they are their mind – they believe that following the mind's images makes them right and being right equals survival for the mind.

This is exactly why people went bananas over the original 13 simple agreements. Their minds were telling them they would not survive under these agreements. Their minds saw the agreements as oppressive. "Show up on time." "Well, what happens if I get stuck in traffic?" The truth is, by taking responsibility we can nearly always be on time. Of course, there are emergencies, but if we want to, we can make our appointments better than 99% of the time. The mind's survival game goes like this: if I agree to be on time, I most likely will feel embarrassed if I am late. To the mind, being embarrassed or humiliated is comparable to dying which, of course, would be the end of the mind's survival game. Panic! Resistance!

In the course they taught that reality is physical and that all reality is based on agreement. I found this part of the training quite compelling. It blew my mind apart! Their notion was that unless a thing was manifested in time, distance – i.e.,. beginning, middle and end; covered or occupied space – and had form; then it didn't exist. Also, for a thing to be real it had to be measurable and testable. For instance, if someone imagined a ten foot rabbit and thought it was real, it wouldn't meet the test of being physical because you couldn't measure it. There was no way to test its reality.

The trainer went on to show how we often depend on an interim test of reality. Some of the interim tests are: authorities, consensus and, if the interim test of reality is reasonable, natural, proper or intrinsically believable. For instance, the difference between the childhood story of the little red chicken who yells, "he sky is falling, the sky is falling," and a group of astronomers who announce that a large asteroid would impact the Earth at 8 P.M. is that the latter is more believable, more reasonable. The essential quality of this interim test of reality is the agreement with scientific authorities would seem more reasonable. It would be reasonable to believe that a group of astronomers "scientific authorities" would know when a large asteroid was going to hit the Earth, but our agreement or disagreement with either of the above two examples is not true until it physically happens. This next example of an agreement is based on a consensus of a randomly selected group of people: If a twelve-person jury *agrees* a defendant is guilty of murder, then their verdict is considered to be legally enforceable and true under the law, and because of their agreement the defendant may lose his or her life. Based on the same evidence, twelve different jurors might *agree* to a verdict of innocent with the accused set free. The reality of a person's guilt or innocence, indeed life or death, is based on a consensus "agreement" of this randomly selected group of individuals. This interim test of reality is said to be true and enforceable under the law, but as we well know, this kind of consensus can result in the death of a innocent person or the freedom of a guilty one.

Still, a problem exists with all reality, including physical reality; not everyone agrees with what is physically real. For instance, scientists agree that light acts like a wave under certain conditions and as a particle under others. Similarly, if you show a photograph to your friends, they will see and agree as to what is in the picture; however, if you show that same picture to certain tribal peoples, they will not be able to see the shapes and forms, or even the outline of the images. Their reality is not in agreement with what we see in the picture, and we may not be able to see some things that they believe are true. Nonetheless, just because we are not in agreement with each other's realities doesn't mean they don't exist.

Reality is in constant flux and is continually evolving. We know this to be true because with every paradigm shift – i.e., the world is flat or the sun revolves around the Earth – when thought and agreement changes, what we believed was real is now altered and reorganized. Therefore what we agree is real today may not be real tomorrow. Thus, reality is all an agreement and illusory. Now, of course, there are all kinds of philosophies that argue many other perspectives. Nevertheless, there is a basic truth to reality being physical, but at the same time being illusory just as light can be both a wave and particle.

If we are not careful, life becomes only a reaction to an externalized reality of a particular era, belief or thought. We become caught in a Have, Do, Be, ass-backwards world of our own creation. For instance, if you want to be an actress, first you *have* to go to acting school and get an acting teacher. Then you *do* as much acting as you can while working your way towards recognition, and perhaps at some point you can *be* an actress. In this kind of system the source of who you are is always outside yourself. While you *try* to accommodate your true being – the source within – to the outside forces, your ability to choose and be responsible is diminished because your focus is external rather than from within. Under those backward circumstances, we are always fighting life, instead of it flowing from our own source. Think of an apple seed trying become an orange tree. Its absurd! An apple seed can not become an orange tree no matter how hard it tries.

When one flows from the source within, an authentic congruency with one's individual truth is established, from which one can move in genuine harmony with all. By starting with who you are, "the Do and the Have" will follow. I am many things, one of which is an actress. I know this as truth, and I have followed this truth on many different life adventures, even though I have not always achieved recognition for it. Being who you are – following the source within – is not always comfortable and can be easily contaminated and misdirected, but as we uncover our source and become aligned with it, the universe will support our truth as we create it in the world. I remember the stories about Werner's search for the truth and the many disciplines he used on that quest. He explored the human potential movement, Zen, and studied with Alan Watts. He was involved with and studied Scientology and Mind Dynamics. One story I remember was when he made a commitment to himself to tell the explicit truth for a whole month. By the end of 30 days, he said, everything seemed to be going his way. He told us that if we continually told the truth, "the way it is," we would be eventually in tune with the universe; however, with each of his disciplines, he said, "as soon as I felt *this is it, I got it*," the harmony of being in accord with the universe would vanish .

Solidifying experiences into images, beliefs and rules of the mind make an individual's awareness one step removed from the moment to moment changing universe, and thus one's awareness becomes distorted and a slave to the mind which colors reality with its own mental structures, misperceptions and lies. For example, in racism the mind colors reality with unexamined mental beliefs, prejudices and concepts which force all individuals within a race or group into broad and unjustified generalizations. Although I have been guilty of stereotyping people, I learned through EST the ability to observe my own prejudices. With conscious awareness and self-observation, I began the process of letting go of these negative mental constructs, which has made my life more open and free of my mind's mentally constructed prison.

These mental prisons are exactly what I experienced in the training. For me, it felt like the trainers set up metaphorical mazes for everyone to run down in search of the truth, to find it, to figure it out. At the end of each maze, there was a wall – a complete dead end and nothing else. After running down these intellectual mazes, you soon understood that trying to find and figure out the truth gets you nowhere. Then you come to the realization that there is nothing "no thing" to get and nowhere "now/here" to be! All reality is just "what it is" and is based on an agreement. There is no ultimate truth. Right then, I realized that I myself was the "source" of my truth and my reality.

After graduating from EST, I spent the next five weeks in relative bliss and peace of mind. However, almost immediately I decided that I wanted to be a trainer. Wow, I thought, for an actress this was the perfect one-person show. Besides, I loved the extemporaneous audience interaction, and I knew that there was a manual and organization to the training which was comparable to a script, which is all any actor needs. Also, I guess I was a lot like my idealist father; I believed in wanting to make the world work for everyone, which was Werner's mission at the time. Anyway, a sold out one-woman performance with audience interaction and service to humanity resonated deeply within my being.

Accordingly, I enrolled in the training program to be a guest seminar leader and later took all seminars and courses required to be a graduate seminar leader. This preparation did lead me to the front of the room in both capacities, and for the next five or six years, as long as I showed up for the agreed upon EST game, my life was fairly blissful. Toward the end, I began to see how the EST organization was operating from a position of survival, especially with how they wanted graduates to continue to enroll in courses without any regard to the individual's life goals and plans outside of EST and the need to get on with one's life. Many of the graduates hid out in EST because in this agreed-upon environment, they felt good about themselves. Eventually, I felt I was hiding out too, so as long as I played their agreed-upon game, I would never know if I could succeed in having a satisfying life for myself. Important to me was creating the necessary aliveness, presence and self-generation that would make life work in the context of my own individual life. Organizations, by their very nature, tend to thwart individual aliveness for the benefits of being organized and having structure.

At that time, Werner's philosophy was to make the world work for everyone. Being of service to humanity was the expressed highest purpose of any individual which, when implemented, made the world work. This philosophy fit well with my dad's social idealism, and being his daughter, the betterment of mankind was also of importance to me. However, implied in being of service as the highest purpose known to man was the corollary that an individual's purpose and needs were secondary.

Later in an advanced seminar, they announced that to be of service was not the highest purpose to life, it was just a game that human beings made up; the highest purpose to life was that *there is no purpose*. This had a ring of truth which I allowed to reverberate into the core of my being. Man is a meaning machine always searching for the meaning in life, and service seems to be the highest and most satisfying form of meaning that man has created. There being no purpose to my life meant that I was responsible for the meaning in my own life. This freed me up because I realized that I was operating in EST out of survival. To serve was doing the right thing, which made me feel good about myself but alienated me from my inner source of who I was. I therefore was stagnating because I was not moving from the creative aliveness within myself but was still trying to compensate my long standing inner defective feelings by following the EST external agreement of being of service, which I unconsciously believed would make me whole.

Through the experience of EST I learned that if I kept my agreements, told the truth, cleaned up my past, and move from the creative source within me, then my life would work. Although my experience with the EST model was exquisitely profound, I now knew that it was time to make a change. My life's cheese was rotten because I was not taking responsibility to choose my own inner meaning. To contribute to life and at the same time fulfill myself had to come from a source within me for it to be valid as an expression of who I was. Werner said that experience is the name of the game; therefore, no matter how profound a system of thought or belief may be, it can cast a dark shadow over your own inner light, diminishing your ability to experience the life force as it uniquely operates through you in the present circumstance of your life. I was stuck in the abstractions and concepts of EST and thus missing out on creating my own life. *So I left EST.*

Leaving EST was like being tossed out of the Garden of Eden. Although I had a bit of the tree of knowledge and had taken a bite of the divine apple, I floundered with the challenge of making my own life work. I was now on my own away from the security of agreed-upon structure and organization. For awhile it was like walking on unsure footing. My insecurity was probably some of my motivation to become involved again in another organized system of learning through experience. Only this time I immersed myself in an organization for actors, The Actors Institute and a course called the Mastery. Nonetheless, my pattern was fully played out as I eventually led the Institute's workshops while running the operation for the Los Angeles branch.

The nine years with both EST and the Mastery was a pattern that needed to be completed while at the same time helping me grow through my many experiences with some great experiential teachers – Werner Erhard being one of the greatest. Now, I am in touch with my own source inside me and finally on my own. By trusting and surrendering to the moment-to-moment process of life, I am taking responsibility for my own choices, whether they work or not.

I have developed several workshops combining all I have experienced and learned with the essence of my own source. My workshop that I facilitate at Esalen Institute, "The Max: Stretching the Limits of Your Self-Expression," is an example of where my experiences, knowledge and essence come together to benefit people from all walks of life.

There are very few things in life that exceed one's expectations. EST was definitely one of those experiences. From the moment the training began, I knew that I was in for a wild ride. I sat in the training room with my mouth hanging open most of the time. It literally blew my mind open and continually amazes me to this day. EST resonated through me with the ring of truth, of what the greater picture really is. It forever transformed the fabric of my life.

Stephen Lewis

E=mc^2

Light is the foundation for all known sentient life. It is through the miracle of light that all life exists, except for a few minor exceptions, as with some bacteria. The Gospel of John made clear the importance of light when it stated, "In him was life and the life was the light of men. The light shines in the darkness, and the darkness has not overcome it."

The scientific fact that energy and matter are directly related is not only expressed through Einstein's equation that energy equals mass times the speed of light squared but is manifested in our daily lives through the wonder of photosynthesis. Without the plant kingdom's ability to convert and store energy from sunlight, life as we know it would vanish. Using a simple analogy, all matter can be viewed as frozen light, meaning that we are beings of light, sustained and fueled by the very light that we are.

My curiosity with energy and how it relates to life began around 1957 in my late teens and early twenties. I was fascinated with the work of Wilhelm Reich, and I eagerly read his books and research. His experiments with orgone energy, and his view that man was a bio-electrical system expanded my outlook by shifting my preconditioned perspectives about humanity. From his years of clinical work as a psychoanalyst, he detailed how the human bio-electrical system functioned within the individual. He showed how the currents of primal libido energy enhanced or debilitated the very nature of human existence, both in the individual and in society at large.

Reich's discovery and experimentation with orgone energy demonstrated a "life force" or energy that was distinct, but not in conflict with other forces within the physical sciences. He discovered this energy through his experiments with bions. Bions are formed by disintegration of organic or inorganic material and, when viewed by a microscope, look like vesicles with a blue colored content. Reich discovered that the bions radiated a form of energy which he called orgone energy. This energy was ubiquitous throughout the universe and was the catalysis for the transition of inorganic matter into the realm of life, as he concluded through his experiments and as stated in his own words:

> *There are certain truths which are a priori given by one's senses and movements. That life, Living, is constant motion, is such a self-evident truth itself. That Love is the merger of two organisms, is another self-evident truth, self-evident from the sense of longing for merger, actual merging and loosing one's circumscribe individual identity during the embrace. That there exists something very alive and emotionally enlivening and vibrating and life-giving in the atmosphere around us, is another self-evident truth, no matter whether it is called God or the Universal Spirit or the Great Father or the Kingdom of Heaven or Orgone Energy.*

It was through my studies in eastern religion and philosophy that I concluded that Reich was dealing with the primal energy known for centuries as prana or chi. Both the Chinese chi and the yogic prana are a subtle nutritive energy that is assimilated into the body through acupuncture meridians, chakras and breath. This energy is essential to life and the functions of a healthy body.

My quest to understand energy as related to life matured, developed and evolved as I studied physics. I was particularly intrigued with the necessity to shift and expand reality to accommodate quantum physics. Even though Newtonian classical physics continues to work well in the macrocosmic world by measuring such an event as the orbit, distance, and position of a telecommunication satellite as well as countless other measurements, it can no longer be considered the basic law of nature as it was once thought to be. Its view of the world as operating like one gigantic predetermined machine is not compatible with subatomic realms, where events were based on probabilities and where an electron behaves in certain situations like a wave and in others like a particle as elaborated in Heisenberg's uncertainty principle.

This shift from the ordinary view of the world spawned new interpretations and theories of reality. Neils Borh, David Bohm, and John Bell were leading physicists who contributed to this new hypothesis founded on the atomic and subatomic realities of quantum physics. Their view sees reality as an interconnected web of things and events that form a unified whole. In such a system, cause and effect are not always easily defined or always observable. Events and matter exist and are influenced at some level by all the forces within the unified whole. Of course, in the everyday world of classical physics, most forces are more predictable than at the level of atoms and electrons, where patterns of probability predominate.

Metaphysical problems for traditional science arise in quantum physics because of the uncertain nature of events and things. This uncertainty, coupled with the view of an interconnected web of reality, suggests that data from observations and experiments are in some way affected by the very scientist who are making the observations and conducting the experiments. In the *Tao of Physics* David Bohm is quoted regarding this interpretation of the universal interconnection of events and matter:

*One is led to a new notion of an unbroken wholeness
which denies the classical idea of analyzability of the
world into separately and independently existing
parts.... We have reversed the usual classical notion
that the independent "elementary parts" of the world
are the fundamental reality, and that the various
systems are merely particular contingent forms and
arrangements of these parts. Rather, we say that
inseparable quantum interconnectedness of the whole
universe is the fundamental reality, and the relatively
independent behaving parts are merely particular and
contingent forms within the whole.*

This universal unity of all events and matter is further
elaborated by Bohm with his hologram analogy. Here Bohm
suggests that each part within the universe somehow contains
the whole. This is similar to the fact that each cell within the
body contains a template for the whole body through DNA
coding, which recently resulted in the cloning of various
animals like Dolly, the first cloned sheep. If we consider light
as the foundation for all life and matter, then we can see how
light as a wave and a particle could be linked into a whole
entwined matrix.

This idea of a living matrix is what every great spiritual
teacher has expressed and known about life, that it exists as a
wave on which all living and inorganic matter are interconnected. This living energy wave is not affected by the everyday considerations of space, time or distance. Within this
universal living matrix all actions and events are instantaneously connected in a dynamic process of change with everything in existence. The image of a large intertwined multi-
leveled cosmic fabric in constant motion comes to mind,
where the ripples of sub waves are distributed throughout the
whole to a lesser or greater extent depending on locality and

accessibility, the latter being most profound when regarded as a doorway of individual human consciousness.

On a practical level, I received several degrees in Oriental medicine and studied homeopathy. Here I learned how subtle energies manifested and worked through the human body. Through my studies, I became aware that the nature of subtle energy is not necessarily revealed through it's physical properties. For instance, homeopathic remedies are created by a process of diluting the medicinal agent to minute or non-existent molecular quantities. All that remains in the remedy is the signature vibration or frequency of the diluted medicinal material. When a needed frequency is applied by way of a homeopathic remedy, equilibrium is restored by allowing a person's bioenergetic system to reestablish and rebalance itself to its natural state. This natural state is where the body's frequencies function normally, which the medical community calls health or the absence of disease symptoms.

From diagnostic equipment like X-rays and C.T. scans to the use of pacemakers, the traditional medical community has explored the use of energy for a long time. In my book, *Sanctuary: The Path to Consciousness,* I reported this example: "Medical researchers working on bone fractures which were having problems mending discovered that they could send an electromagnetic signal to the fracture to stimulate rapid healing. It seems that the electromagnetic frequency was carrying the same message as a chemical produced by the body."

As years passed, I continued to explore the essential nature and qualities of energy through physics, Oriental medicine, homeopathy, and mysticism. During the same time period, I also became extremely interested in computers and the technology that made them possible. About 1984, during my employment as a computer consultant, I became aware of some individuals using computers to determine frequency imbalances within the body. The frequencies were determined by measuring the variances in electromagnetic changes of the subtle energy in the acupuncture meridian system. These variances indicated health or pathology for the underlying organs of the meridian being tested. Later, I learned of some rudimentary computerized systems that attempted to use a combination of energy and consciousness to determine frequency imbalances within the body. Although these were very early and unrefined attempts, I understood the vast and basically untapped potential of computer systems to assess and restore frequency imbalances.

The development of my own computer system has been a continuum of conscious advancements, as has been the case with my own developing individual consciousness. My idea of consciousness is different than most people. To most people consciousness is defined by what they are aware of and can articulate. I see consciousness as incorporating all aspects of the greater selfhood, whether or not this information is contained in personal knowing. All healing is self-healing, which is accomplished by focusing and channeling one's own life force energy. Consciousness is that focus whether or not the personal self knows it. Consciousness is the total informational system being applied and focused to one's life circumstance as it is needed. This includes personal knowledge but goes far beyond it.

Consciousness is multidimensional with the personal self often being the last aspect to know the specifics of anything. This certainly has been the case with the challenges and obstacles I encountered through the ongoing development of my frequency and consciousness based computer technology. Before crucial solutions reveal themselves to me, I often reach a point of desperation. During such times, I usually return to the solitude and peace of the desert, where a source of wisdom larger than I am often reveals a new and grander solution to the problem at hand. In *Sanctuary: The Path To Consciousness*, I reported about one such crucial turning point and the important transformative experience that accompanied my trek into what is often considered a wasteland:

I had climbed to a picturesque mountaintop where I had planned to camp the night. While watching the sunset's golden light cast shadows over the basin below, I became hyperaware of my surroundings, as if the distinction between myself and the scenic environment had melted away. I was the sunset. I was the wind. I was the rocks, and yet I was still uniquely me. I closed my eyes to envision an image of an eagle soaring above me. When I opened my eyes, I saw an eagle circling overhead, which engendered a feeling of protection. A sense of being watched caused my head to turn automatically, revealing two gazing eyes of a nearby mountain lion. Now eye to eye, the mountain lion gently lay down as the eagle flapped its mighty wings, perching itself onto an adjacent rock. Awed and overwhelmed by this spectacular wonder, I looked down at my hand clutching a fistful of sand which I slowly let sift back to the ground. In that instant, I knew the solution to the energetic problem I'd been trying to solve. I knew how to measure and affect the subtle energetic essence that mystics had talked about for thousands of years and how it was connected to electricity and atomic forces.

Through the unity of the moment, I heard the eagle and mountain lion say that my destiny was to help others, and that at the right time I would be led to share this knowledge in a growing community. This community was to be incorporated into a church.

Of course, the idea of a church was consistent with what I had learned through many years of self-development; that you can't separate science, philosophy and religion. Since everything is energy, then all fields of knowledge must coalesce and be unified. I speak to this reality in my book: "Spirit is energy and energy is spirit. $E=mc^2$. Thus all illness is spiritual, which is to say all illness is energetic in nature. Dis-ease is due to an individual's misalignment with the power of the spiritual energy within them and which is around them. By realigning the individual to be in harmony with the spiritual force, the life force, the subtle energetic matrix that makes up the entire universe, that individual's physical, emotional, and even spiritual ailments will disappear."

However, I *do not* perform medical treatments or diagnosis with my computer system. I do not ask about symptoms, make physical examinations, measure pulse or take blood samples. I do not in anyway treat anyone's disease or disease symptoms. I work with subtle energies and detect energetic signatures or frequencies using my technologically advanced computer system. By imprinting subtle energetic frequencies and using holographic technology, the individual's own subtle life force and organizing principle reestablishes harmony and balance within the person's body, emotions and spirit. If others would like to label this has health or the absence of disease, I can only say that is their right to speak as they believe. Since I can not confirm the connection between frequencies and actual disease manifestations, I can only say that if an individual has cancer, AIDS or other frequencies that we have identified and he or she experiences the disease being eliminated through our work, then they must have experienced a spontaneous healing. For me to make any other claim would be illegal and unethical, because the disease process is the domain of the medical community. I can only say that in our church of many faiths, spiritual and spontaneous healings are common occurrences for our members.

George Bernard Shaw said, "The reasonable man adapts himself to the world. The unreasonable man persists in trying to adapt the world to himself. Therefore all progress depends on the unreasonable man."

Since everything is energy and all consciousness is a continuum of progress, I can not envision a time where I would be satisfied being a reasonable man. It is opposite to my own intrinsic nature. In one sense, faith is the trust and belief in what seems unreasonable. St. Augustine said, "Miracles occur, not in opposition to nature, but in opposition to what we know of nature." Our knowledge of nature's universe has barely scratched the surface. I see myself as on a continuum of ever increasing consciousness concerning the knowledge and application of energy.

In regards to the computer/consciousness system we use today: I see it as far more accurate than it was a year ago, and I certainly expect the system next year to transcend what it is today. I can't conceive of my work ever stopping, because with energy anything is possible. I have a fantasy that in the moment before I die I will sit up and say, "I got it together!" I realize that only an unreasonable man could dream of such a thing and have the daring and heart to work towards it.

Surrender Your Illusion of Power

Listening to the song "Done too Soon" by Neil Diamond, I heard a number of famous names sung in succession. As names like Marilyn Monroe, Ghengis Khan, Humphrey Bogart, Buster Keaton, Jesus Christ, Fanny Brice, Graham Bell and the Marx's brothers, were sung, I began to realize that all the people named were dead. These people "sweated under the same sun and marveled under the same moon" and in the end "it was all done too soon." This song is a great illustration of personal power and the many forms that it takes through famous persons. It demonstrates that power held by human beings always ends and is constrained by time. Is nothing forever?

Life is in an ever-changing flux. Power and the powerful are ever changing, shifting and transforming with the passage of time. Thus power is a temporal illusion of life. Today's powerful and the use of their power are but tomorrow's memories. This basic life truth, when examined, cannot be denied. With the passage of time, it continually calls us to adjust and move towards its salient and revealed wisdom.

In our lives we exercise great power. We turn the light switch and the light comes on. We turn the key and the car engine starts. We turn on the faucet and water pours out of the pipe. These are some examples of power which we often take for granted. All acts of mastery, simple, common or complex, influence the psyche consciously, or unconsciously, in a belief of personal power. This fact is easily noticed when my car won't start, or the light doesn't come on. As reality hits me straight in the face, I can easily become frustrated as my unconscious belief in my personal power is challenged.

Otherwise, my reaction would be to accept the situation and do the best I can.

Power can be negatively held also. A woman or man might say, "I have never been successful in relationships with the opposite sex." This illustrates a negative powerful belief that inhibits the success of acquiring the necessary skills. We learn who we are through our many life experiences. These tend to solidify into concrete personal identities, and positions of power over ourselves, life and its events.

We seek personal power to avoid the discomforts in life. When we can have power over people, places and things we don't have to feel our pain, insecurity or loneliness. We can deny that life, our lives, are very vulnerable. We avoid or suppress the fact that in life there are no safe havens from the ravages of time and change.

Another problem with power is that it is unconsciously habitual. Pavlov, the famous Russian psychologist, demonstrated how powerful experiential learning can affect behavior. He conditioned a dog to salivate at the ring of a bell. He did this by pairing the ring with the delivery of food. Soon the dog would salivate to the ring even if no food was presented and would continue to respond without food for many trials. This is interesting?

The power of habit is profound even when it is ineffectual. How many times do we repeat the same behavior, expecting different results each time? The bells of our conditioning ring a negative tune, and we jump into the boiling caldron.

I believe all sense of human power is temporal. It only exists in time. This is simply illustrated by observing how time affects life and all human endeavors. We build a house, and there is power in that structure. It protects us from the elements; but as time moves on, the house declines in power to perform its function. Similarly, we build psychic structures in our minds, often to protect ourselves from early trauma. These psychic structures and images cannot meet the ever changing challenges of life and development because they lack the fluidity needed to accommodate different circumstances . To be stuck in an outdated structure of power can be very painful and unrewarding.

Powerlessness, surrender and acceptance are not words that are leading us toward helplessness or complacency. These are words suggesting the need to review outdated psychic power structures, so we can evaluate their effectiveness in the present. In our culture, the quest for power to compensate for early trauma is enormous, but so often we are just salivating to things, people and psychic beliefs that no longer have any food to sustain and nurture us.

Jesus communicated the need to surrender the illusion of power with the words in a well-known parable, "if ye have faith as a mustard seed." The traditional interpretation is that even faith as small as a mustard seed can grow larger. A Buddhist would see the same saying in a different light. Faith is represented here, but it is the faith of the seed to die, to surrender its power, so the next stage of growth can take place. If the seed were able to hold on to its power of being a seed, the mustard plant and all its growth and development would only be a potential one.

So what to do with personal power? The power we can utilize to affect life, ours and others'.

This question, for each person, must be answered on an individual basis. Since the answer changes within the context and passages our lives, it is important to set aside time for solace and reflection on a regular basis. By doing so, we can stay in touch with what is important in our present life circumstances. With the goal of taking care of ourselves and our families, we certainly want to be meaningfully productive while enjoying our life to the fullest. Still, we must remember that most accomplishments will fade with the passage of time. What remains are our true gifts, our offerings that nurture life itself. Qualities like compassion, patience, courtesy, gentleness, humility, and love become our true gifts because they endure through time by touching and nurturing other human beings who, in turn, can touch and nurture. By grace and the use of positive human qualities, man and individual man evolve and become whole.

Is nothing forever? It is not money, fame, status or control that endure, only our affect on the human spirit.

Power and powerlessness must be viewed in a new light. We must realize the world is seducing us to believe we are powerful. It can be as subtle as the turning of a key; compelling with the seduction of mass advertisement, fulfilling with the mastery of skills or a negative powerful believe about oneself. Still, personal power is illusory because it diminishes with the passage of time. To move toward our next level of development, we must give up the illusion of power by focusing on the qualities of our humanity that transcend time.

The next chapter, "A Thing Is What It Is," explores human nature. By using our divine gifts, we can increasingly move towards greater avenues of expression and being.

A Thing is What it is

On the surface the statement "A thing is what it is" seems simple, like the logical mathematical equation A=A. In the material world, we learn quite young the functions of most things. We know that a pencil is for writing and shoes are worn to protect our feet, and once an object's function is learned, it is seldom used for any other purpose.

On occasion, however, we see things being used for purposes outside their original function. For instance, pencils being used as drum sticks and shoes as flying objects of contempt. Instantaneously, the mind can creatively transform objects into new uses by knowing the qualities and characteristics of the things being transformed. This creative process happens all the time. Seemingly, man's imagination and creativity has unlimited ability to transform the material plane. Being open and seeing an object's or an idea's unique characteristics while creatively blending them into something new is all that is required.

Human beings are much more complex. In addition to our physical bodies, we have an infinite variety of functions, characteristics, and qualities. We are constantly being impacted by internal and external forces and stimuli that sway our emotions, thinking, perceptions, and spiritual understandings. Different worlds are created and vanish moment to moment. For example, when I am angry a completely different person seemingly exists than when I am meditating.

Despite the many forces impacting our lives, free will is said to be the basis of our ability to make choices, but Man's free will is often just an illusion driven by unconscious patterns and habits which constrict our lives into very narrow ways of living and being. An unconscious life is closed and static and allows nothing fundamentally new to be introduced. Even the most arduous seekers of self-understanding and truth must deal with the enormous power of habitual patterns. As a psychotherapist, I know this to be true in both the lives of my clients and in my own life. Like driving on automatic pilot, habitual patterns are rote and unconscious, making change difficult if not impossible. Considering the forces pushing us toward limited avenues of expression and behavior, it's amazing that fundamental change can take place at all. The image of an hourglass comes to mind, the sand having only one way to go.

Is life truly this limiting? Consider this Zen story. A long time ago there was a monk who lived high in a mountaintop monastery. After a week of rain, the clouds parted and the sun came out. Feeling restless, the monk decided to take a walk and breathe in the sweet-smelling fresh air. He walked down a well-traveled path enjoying the afterglow of the rain-drenched forest and came to a large puddle with a scorpion thrashing about in eminent danger of drowning. With great compassion the monk bent down and gently picked up the scorpion. As he placed it on dry ground, the scorpion stung him and ran back into the puddle. Being compassionate the monk once more picked up the scorpion and was stung again while placing him on dry land, only to have the scorpion run back into the puddle. This scene repeated several times before the monk noticed a wise old man watching. The monk by this time was pretty exasperated and asked the old man why the scorpion had continued to sting him when he was only trying to help. The old man calmly said, "It's in the nature of the scorpion to sting."

Does our nature truly limit the choices in our lives? The answer is definitely yes, especially for those who do not seek to live consciously. In Brugh Joy's book, *Joy's Way*, he states that psychologists believe people to be 20% aware and 80%

unaware of their actions and motivations, but he suggests that a more realistic figure is 0.0001% awake, and over 99% unaware. Since the publication of his book over two decades ago, individual awareness has been helped through the great advantages of mass media, such as radio therapy talk shows, self-help books and educational programs on P.B.S. and cable television. Nonetheless, I believe most behaviors and motives are substantially unconscious in the form of unconscious patterns.

When we are fully involved in our lives, it's hard to believe that our choices aren't based on free will; however, a review of the forces impinging on free will might change your mind. Take for instance a story that I heard in graduate school. I cannot attest to its validity, but as a behavioral therapist, the story is easy to believe based on the power of reward and punishment on behavior. The story as told to me was about a professor specializing in behavioral learning who knew about the power of stimulus-response, reward and punishment. Apparently, he walked back and forth in front of his class while lecturing. His students decided to put him on a schedule of reward and punishment. Every time he walked to the left, they became inattentive, ruffled papers, and coughed. In contrast, when he walked from the center to the right they gave him their undivided attention. Before long, as the story goes, he was only walking on the right side of the room back and forth within a two-foot range.

Unconsciously, we most often move towards the pleasant and avoid the disagreeable. In the above story, it is obvious that attention was rewarding for the professor, and powerful enough to unconsciously and dramatically change his behavior. The overwhelming scientific evidence is that we are conditioned from birth, and that conditioning substantially affects our behavior. In the case of the professor, his two-foot walking range would continue so long as he was unconscious of the student's reinforcement; he would be subject to further conditioning of his attention needs in similar circumstances. Thus, the range of one's actions and behaviors is limited by one's conditioning.

As with behavioral conditioning, unresolved pain engenders patterned behavior. Reacting, adjusting, denying and compensating are some of the many ways in which the push and pull of core selfhood injuries impact behavior, character, and attitudes. Our psyches are designed to defend against being injured or reinjured, often resulting in automatic behaviors and actions that can be self-defeating. For example, I used to get very upset and essentially throw a tantrum whenever I spilled food or drink. The behavior of throwing things and stomping around wasted more energy and time than merely cleaning it up. My core emotional injury and self-image ruled my behavior until, through self-examination, I was able to change. Unfortunately, most unconscious, unresolved injury patterns are far more insidious because they are much less obvious. One can defend a core emotional injury with an automatic reactive pattern throughout a lifetime and be unaware of the pattern or even the reaction.

How fragile our egos are! How easy it is to avoid and deny characteristics about ourselves. How easy it is to defend ourselves against further injuries. The ability of the psyche and personality to defend themselves is very broad in range. A list of some common defense mechanisms includes: denial, fantasy, repression, suppression, rationalization, protection, reaction formation, displacement, emotional insulation, intellectualization, repression, identification, introjection, compensation and acting-out.

Habits and conformity are other ways we restrict free will. A habit is like a well worn path in the jungle. It gets us where we want to go quickly, but limits all other possible avenues and experiences to that single path.

How much do habits reduce free will and choice? If you take just one hour out of your waking day and really observe your behavior and actions you'll probably be amazed. We work, eat, socialize, recreate, dress, worship, clean, think and feel in very predictable ways. For instance, watch yourself dress in the morning. Is there a routine and habit to it? Do you bathe first or eat first? When you come home from work, what is the first thing you typically do? Is it automatic? I think as you observe yourself you'll see how automatic many behaviors are. We get into a groove, seldom deviating because of past choices, ease, and familiarity. For many of us, habits are so ingrained and unconscious that they do not change one iota throughout life. Again, this restricts us from being present, alert and alive, which in turn limits our choices to the habit or routine at hand.

By way of reason, man can be aware of his own life and living experiences. By the same gift of reason he can know his own separateness and differences. There is a primordial fear associated with being separate and different, out of which arises a need for conformity and a predisposition towards a herd instinct and psychology. In the primitive jungle, encountering something that was different could mean one was about to be eaten. This innate fear of difference is manipulated by institutions, religions, families, governments, and especially the mass media. Every form of advertisement lures one at some level to be like someone else, which assuages the fear of difference. If you use such-and-such shampoo, you will be beautiful and sexy just like the model in the ad. It was a shock to me in the '60s with my long hair and love beads to be told how conforming I was. The amount of conformity is reflected in the proliferation of emblems, sports shirts, corporate seals and insignias so common today.

Conformity engenders a comfortable feeling of similarity which relieves the inborn fear of difference, but with conformity and "sameness" comes the forfeiture of God's great gift to life, the rare precious individual that you are, as unique as your fingerprint.

Conditioning, habits, patterns and emotional injuries constrict and color our experiences, behaviors, and motivations, but our five senses limit our awareness even more. Our senses are very ineffective in actually perceiving reality. In fact, if we were aware of all sensory stimuli, we would be so overwhelmed as to be totally helpless. Our five senses dramatically reduce the kinds of information reaching our brains by their simple limitations, and the brain sets up models of reality to simplify the vast amount of data it receives, eliminating stimuli outside those models as irrelevant. In fact, what we believe we perceive are just functional imitations of reality. They are very good approximations but still imitations that often cause misperceptions of what is actually real. Studies show that expected and familiar images are perceived much more quickly than uncommon ones; they fit the created models of the brain. For example, an experimental group was briefly shown a set of playing cards in which a few aces of spades were painted red. When the participants were asked how many aces of spades were included in the deck, they gave low estimates because the deceptive red cards did not fit the ordinary model of playing cards and were not perceived and counted.

Often our world is a simple reflection of what we think, feel and believe it should be. For instance, one's mood can influence how we see the world. When we're in a good mood everything seems rosy and when our mood is bad even beneficial things are colored negative. Likewise when we are angry, other people seem irritable or angry themselves. Most of us have experienced the closed-mindedness of religious zealots or the euphoric perceptions of someone totally swept away by love.

External life circumstances change so rapidly it gives the illusion that individuals are changing too. Our body changes as we grow older, new things are invented, and political structures come and go, but who we are fundamentally never changes dramatically unless significant effort is placed in knowing oneself. The old saying "physician heal thyself" is significant when applied to anyone on this quest for wholeness, with conscious self-knowledge its cornerstone. Self-knowledge and then acceptance are required before there can be change, especially fundamental change, which can only be accurately measured by comparing an individual to himself.

"A thing is what it is" implies some important attributes about human life. To a great extent most people operate within given parameters. As pointed out in our previous discussion, people are who they are and can be nothing else without self-examination. This fact can give one a sense of peace, freedom, and acceptance toward one's fellow human beings knowing that in any given moment a person can be only who he or she is. When a person depreciates or injures others, his actions reflect his unconscious attitudes, character, and injury patterns, and usually when we are annoyed or reactive to such an individual's behaviors, we announce our own unconscious patterns.

In the unified or whole state of consciousness there are few if any unresolved personal dynamics. One who moves from a unified state of consciousness can be very confrontational, as was Christ with the Pharisees, but such actions are with the intent and aim of greater consciousness and wholeness and exclude personal issues related to self-will, fear, control and power.

So often we have images in our minds about the way we want our life to be. When we begin to abandon and surrender these life illusions and fantasies, a sense of deep awe and appreciation will manifest with a growing sense of gratitude and peace for each of our experiences. Each experience, whether appearing positive or negative, moves us toward the tapestry of wholeness: the only difference between stumbling blocks and stepping stones is in the way we use them.

Again, the first step in the creative process is to know and be aware of the attributes and characteristics of the thing, idea or individual being changed. For human beings this requires a great undoing, a great unraveling of the deep mysteries of the small self yielding to the unified integrated Self . If you are not doing the work needed for conscious living you are stuck in the mire of conditioning, habit, and fantasy. The needle in the haystack can usually only be found by slowly removing each blade of hay.

At any given moment, "life is what it is." There is a *suchness* quality to life that goes beyond our attempts to dominate and control it. Like a cool breeze or the warmth of a friendly hug, life's river flows. The forces in life can be powerful enough to move a mountain or gentle enough to caress a child's cheek , but life was never intended to be contained , only appreciated and experienced.

I am that I am, the image of God in the Bible, suggests a comforting realization that God can not be changed by the small self, the self of conditioning, habit, and narcissistic fantasy. God can not be accessed at the level of automatic patterned behavior or thought. Only with an open, unencumbered, unbiased and clear conscious state of being can God be experienced.

We can experience God, who is ever-present, with wisdom and grace! Mystics throughout the ages and in a variety of cultures have reported similar experiences of God's knowable attributes. Although there are some differences in these mystical experiences that can be attributed to culture, age, and geographical location, their fundamental qualities are the same. The most important of these are the understanding and appreciation that the ultimate reality is beyond the perception of the senses and is unified in all things. This unity in all things, or oneness, is beyond all reason and unifies the duality between seer and the seen without the use of sensual perception. Although all mystical experiences do not contain this characteristic of oneness, they have some quality that moves toward it, such as clarity in Ray's story.

The transformational stories in this book illuminate some of the wide variety of divine awareness and/or experience that one can have by seemingly chance circumstances or volitional acts of conscious self-will. Often present in these experiential stories are the qualities of humility within the circumstance, strong authentic feelings, a feeling of yielding or surrender, and a vulnerable openness. Where self-will is utilized, the qualities of discipline and a motivation to profoundly know oneself are present. These experiences transform the static-closed attitudes, characteristics, and even conditioning into a new light and way of being.

A transformational experience can initiate one on a quest of self-development, forming a deepening spiritual relationship and identity, as was the case in many of these stories. In a moment of time or a lifetime of arduous labor, one can be transformed with the small self yielding its illusory place of dominance and power for a unified state and experience. Often this is a slow process with the ego letting go in small degrees, or it can happen in a dramatic event moving the ego closer towards wholeness and unification. This yielding does not diminish the importance of the small self but merely

aligns individual experiences of life in some way to the unified reality.

What is arrogance? "It is being oblivious and insensible
to what is essential," as stated by Melvana Jalalludin Rumi.

If the forces of life are towards a pre-determined existence, then mediocrity and complacency could be accepted as
the natural rule to follow, but the fact that human beings can
reason and be self-aware places humanity at the acme of
known life. As pointed out in the last chapter on external
power, most created structures and ideas cannot stand against
the test of time, but with our ability to share and communicate our awareness and consciousness, humanity can transmit
the wonders of being present, alive, self-aware, spiritually
whole and self-responsible through modeling, as have all the
great spiritual teachers. It is our human responsibility to become self-aware. Otherwise, the unity and beauty of humanity is lost in unconscious determinism, and individuals remain
stagnant and closed.

At this time we cannot presuppose that everyone has
equal ability and opportunity to address this Herculean task
of self-awareness. In fact, we are all in various developmen-
tal stages with the vast majority of humanity not engaged in
knowing themselves beyond rudimentary levels. Most people
of the world are simply trying to maintain existence. A sense
of compassion can be released from the depths of our being,
knowing that each of us struggle against our own closed psychological systems – endeavoring to develop harmony, balance and wholeness as best we can. At the same time there is
nothing greater than this struggle. Jesus says in Chapter 8 of
Mark, " For what does it profit a man, to gain the whole
world and forfeit his life." True choice, true life comes from
the depths of self-awareness, which leads to a sublime state
of being.

The inherent predetermined qualities of human life can engender a sense of real freedom, a freedom from reaction. The following story illustrates this point: A guru and his disciple were walking in a crowded marketplace when a man ran up to them cursing and chastising them as charlatans. When the man left, the disciple asked, "How could you allow this man to embarrass you in front of all these people?" "What do you mean, embarrass me?" said the guru, "that man was showering me with love."

Human beings are too often absorbed by the small self's desires, opinions, thoughts, patterns and emotions. As we grow in self-awareness and expanded consciousness, our prejudicial view of life and one's limiting patterns are placed into a new perspective. This allows an acceptance and yielding to the life's direction in the here and now. We begin accepting the nature of people, thoughts, ideas and things as they are: "a thing is what it is." This begins the freeing of unconscious patterns as revealed by one's reactions. Unconscious patterns are revealed by one's reactivity just as a doorbell announces a guest. Freeing ourselves from reactive patterns is one of the first steps towards wholeness and unity. As we become self-aware, our precious life force is released towards creative endeavors.

Every year I plant a vegetable garden in my back yard. Occasionally a tomato seed will stick at the top of the sink's drain grate and sprout a root several inches down the pipe. Often when this happens the seedling will still have its husk around the head of the seed, for there is no soil in the sink to dislodge it. I know from experience in my garden that without dislodging the husk the seed is doomed for death.

People, places, and things are the soil of our existence and maturation. We are constantly rubbing up against the conflicts generated in this crucible. Introspective reflection is one major path toward engendering peace and serenity, the catalyst and glue for wholeness. Releasing reactivity signals the softening and eventual surrender of personal patterns and prejudicial views that color most of our actions and motivations. Out of this come avenues to access the infinite silence from where manifestation originates and out of which creation and creativity abounds.

Seek the kingdom of God and everything else will be given unto you. Many think the kingdom of God is a place with a definite location and ambiance. My belief is that it is a state of being where the individual is unclouded by personal patterns and motivations. Where God and a sentient being creatively interact, moving creation towards ever-expanded awareness and unified wholeness. The glory of this motion towards wholeness overshadows the illusory quest for personal achievement, power, and dominance. It really is the only game that can with stand the changing forces of time. After being asked by the Pharisees when the kingdom of God was coming, Jesus answered, "The kingdom of God is not coming with signs to be observed; nor will they say 'Lo, there it is!' or 'There' for behold, the kingdom of God is in the midst of you."

What is needed is a conscious effort at creating new ways of being out of what exists in us now. That is, the characteristics and attitudes that push and influence our lives today. Through self-awareness, yielding, and God's grace, the creative nature of God can come into play. As we open to the divine by yielding our self-direction and will, the interplay and interaction can reconfigure, add and/or subtract from what already exists to manifest something completely new. Seemingly paradoxical, true change – lasting change – is a function of God's grace and self-awareness which creates a new perspective of life through divine inspiration.

One answer to life's mysteries is to search for the truth within oneself. This is an arduous task of undoing and becoming. This quest leads to a sense of peace and serenity within the frame of wholeness. Here, individuals can be in the midst of the kingdom, creatively enhancing the value of human existence while the divine plays life's array of colors through them.

Faith to be Human

Life's journey is not easy. The challenge of being open is daunted by many forces, and disregarding aspects of ourselves is extremely easy. To be totally aware of all of the forces which impact us is beyond human capability, calling into question the quantity and quality of human free will. Included in all the limitations constricting human free will is the fact that God, the Other, through the unconscious and external world is an integral part of each life, thing, and action. As the mystics describe, everything and everyone is unified in God, the Other, and at the same time separate. A bubble on a ocean of water illustrates the idea how one can be unified and separate, with separation being both real and illusory. The ability to consciously live this paradox is an awesome task.

One can assume that free will was never meant to be absolute. No matter what power a human ego may possess, it is limited within time and space. In this space-time reality, human power is never absolute and is always transitory. When we consider that today's powerful individuals are tomorrow's old, infirmed or vanquished, we know that ultimately human beings are powerless. Even in our daily lives, events continually take place that lack our immediate control. Nonetheless, our greatest responsibility is utilizing our human power to complete ourselves while benefiting all. This can be accomplished through our communion with and direction from an inner resource, the ever-present universal love and oneness.

Unfortunately, with the ever-increasing stimuli of man-made technology, our focus can easily be absorbed in our daily lives excluding the moment-to-moment fact that God, the Other, is our ultimate and only provider. We are dependent for all the living essentials on a mystery that is a part of ourselves, yet separate and unknowable. This seems absurd in our daily lives as we exercise our self-will to meet our goals, desires and needs. Yet, as in the example of the bubble-ocean metaphor, our ego-personality is feeble compared to the resources of the ocean. Still, we must remember that our spirit-essence transcends all worldly limitations because its quality is made from God's basic nature.

Human life is supported by and unified within the Other's collective ocean. In our separateness, we have forgotten this essential fact and live our lives in self-generated illusions. These illusions and daily dreams are built one upon another until the reservoir of our true life, our true nature is but a distant memory. Yet the Other is ever-present and peacefully waiting to be remembered and recognized.

We have explored in previous chapters the limitations of human free will. There should be no doubt that free will is not a solid factor in many life actions. It is important, however, to realize that free will is a function of the amount of consciousness that one possesses. In fact real choice is the ability to assess – with a conscious level of awareness, intelligence, wisdom and understanding the – many complex forces that affect important decisions. However, since many of these forces are beyond the limits of the ego to assess, individuals are limited to the extent by which they can commune with the collective forces of God, the Other upon which we are all dependent. This communion opens up greater resources than are available to the ego. In the information age, it's like being connected to the Internet.

Unfortunately, most of humanity identifies itself with its individual bubble rather than the ocean upon which it rests. The individual-God axis is dominated by the ego-personality which subordinates God, the Other, to segmented parts of life: church, meditation, contemplation, reading scriptures and spiritual fellowship. During these reflective times, the truth of our servitude to the demands, desires and distortions of our ego-personality is sometimes glimpsed; however, the enormity of the ocean-bubble metaphor is quickly forgotten in the hustle and bustle of daily life.

From our earliest days, subtle and overt demands and expectations are placed upon us by our parents, school , friends, church and other significant social forces and institutions. Attitudes, behaviors, and self-beliefs develop from our adaptations to these implied and overt social rules and dictates. For example, in the past we commonly heard "little boys don't cry" and "girls don't get angry." Now, gender differences are being minimized and unisex is stressed. Still, although these societal norms and pressures are significant, they are less substantial when compared to the adaptations caused by family rules and stress, which often squelch our innate potential and true self. Jung said that the first major accomplishment in life was to solve our father-mother complexes. In my family the saying "blood is thicker than water" meant no matter how we abuse each other that we should always stick together. Even when a family supports individuality, adaptation still takes place which produces separation and fragmentation within the individual. For example, men and women will behave differently in mixed gender social situations than within their same-sex groups, such as when men exchange humor about women while watching sports or when women's conversations drift towards the men in their lives. Unity within ourselves and the whole of creation is lost to the forces of separation as our true Self, never yet realized, continues to be displaced by a life of separation. The consciousness of Unity and the One is lost to the dominance of I am: a man, a woman, a Christian, a Buddhist, intelligent, rich, poor, handsome, ugly, strong, weak, and on and on....

Re-membering, bringing together the fragmented parts of ourselves, helps unify our individuality. Increased knowledge of oneself augments the Self, a unifying force within the psyche. This engenders humility as we see ourselves more clearly in juxtaposition to the grandeur of the One. In the bubble-ocean metaphor, the bubble is now conscious of being separate yet One, which frees life's energy for creativity and communion with the source of all. Every separate part of creation is now known to be the greater One. Great love, honor, compassion and serenity are now awakened.

As a boy, one of my friend's favorite recreations was building jigsaw puzzles. His sister gave him a gift of a beautiful 500-piece Springbok German puzzle. He spent a number of evenings putting this puzzle together. As the puzzle's finish grew near, his whole family crowded around the table to lend a hand in the completion. As the last apparent piece was placed into its appropriate spot, they all noticed that a piece somewhere in the middle was missing. The puzzle, a striking resemblance of the boy King Tutankhamen, was now imperfect. They all searched everywhere and finally found the piece on the floor under the sofa. Soggy, stained and discolored, the missing piece was pressed and molded into its designated spot – his dog's contribution to the puzzle. As they stood back to admire their elegant masterpiece, everyone's focus continued to gaze at the little flawed shape on Tutankhamen's right cheek. Hard as they tried, their perception of the whole picture was lost to the ruined piece, the part that stood out as different.

A jigsaw puzzle is a finished product which is then cut into many pieces. Already complete, it started as a whole before being sectioned. Just as a seed of a giant redwood has all its potential locked within a small structure, all human beings have unique potentials and possibilities locked within their psyches. As with any seed, our potential is born to a particular ground. Along with the terrain of a certain family, culture, and community, we inherit inclinations towards talents, characteristics and qualities which all combine into a unique and unrivaled person. As we develop and mature, our potentials either lie dormant or flower in the ambiance of a loving environment. Most often, these innate creative promises are restricted by our human circumstances. For example, a father may want his son to work in his business rather than pursue his artistic talent or, worse yet, the talents are squashed in the chaos of an alcoholic home. Just as in a dense forest a tree must grow thin and tall to compete for the available sunlight, we often succumb to the external forces that limit our inherent potentials.

Most people see themselves as a person with a soul or spirit, but really we are spiritual beings in a human form. How could it be any other way, knowing that every individual is part of the greater One. Typically, the unrestrained human ego, small self, is inclined towards self-importance and inflation. This inflated state can manifest itself in either positive or negative traits and behaviors. For instance, statements like: I will save the hungry masses from starving, or I will conquer the whole world for God's glory, originate from the self-important ego when they exclude divine inspiration and communion. Although many human egos have portrayed themselves as God-like, these representations are always illusory and lack true access to God's resources. When the ego surrenders or yields its dominant position to the Self, a higher developed part of the human psyche, then a human-God relationship can take place. This relationship is the key to a true spiritually fulfilling life. No matter what social status a person has: janitor, baker, teacher, doctor, if the ego yields to the Self, the human-God integration of will and energy is creatively combined and manifested.

A new partnership is forged – the individual now places himself within the wider perspective of the divine. "A thing is what it is" means a full acceptance of oneself within the grander perspective of God as everyone, and everything. Acceptance is now the first step towards harmony – within oneself the coalescing of the separate forces is enhanced by the divine essence of serenity and peace, an inherent quality of God. Experiencing the divine perspective illuminates the one-sided or ego nature of our constricting beliefs, attitudes and actions. As we yield and accept "what is," our lives run smoother because our beliefs and thoughts are in less conflict with our true reality.

The store-house of beliefs, thoughts, and agreements about ourselves and others exclude the grander perspective and make this new partnership hard to maintain. For instance, what is prejudice but an agreement to see someone as different and separate from oneself. The Irish Catholics and Protestants are good examples. Their age old agreements, handed down for generations, lock them into actions that exclude the fact that they both believe in the love of Christ. Once you make an agreement about another person, a group of people, or yourself, the accuracy of that belief is seldom questioned because our beliefs and thoughts color reality, and we see these distortions reflected back as valid.

When I was a child, my father verbally abused me regarding my disability. As a child I had no defense against these wounding words, and they went deep within the core of my being – as truth. I constructed agreements and beliefs about myself regarding my differences and limitations based on the feelings and thoughts of a man who was out of control. These childhood beliefs and agreements have dogged me most of my life. Although it is important to acknowledge the reality of my limitations and differences – "a thing is what it is" – my childhood wounded beliefs and agreements exclude the divine perspective of wholeness and unity, and force me to live in a world of self-generating shame and inadequacy. With much time and effort, my childhood beliefs and agreements are less intense. I more often allow the truth of divine unity in seeing myself and others. God does not see man-woman, black-white, healthy-unhealthy, night or day. This is the world of separation. God's very essence is the reality of wholeness, unity, and love. When the bubble on the ocean breaks, nothing is lost except the temporary illusion of separation. However, much is gained by bringing into this world of illusions the unity, wholeness and love of God. To see with fresh eyes is to see "what is," knowing that it is made with the substances and spark of the divine.

Being in harmony with everyone and everything seems like an impossibility, especially from the ego's invested belief system. However, in our individual daily lives the more we are capable of being in tune and in balance with divine wisdom, peace, and unity the easier life flows. This is not easy to manifest or even judge accurately. Still, we know that ego-willed actions and demands can cause disharmony within ourselves and with those to whom we relate mutually. A disharmonious split occurs within our psyche when we either exercise ego power demands or acquiesce to such demands, ignoring our own best interest. Active or passive display of self-willed ego power originates from early-on beliefs and agreements about ourselves. Such displays of power always exclude the active communion and participation of the divine.

Recently, I invited some developmentally disabled clients to my home for pizza and a movie. At the pizza parlor, the owner had just opened for business and looked tired. He asked if I could come back in an hour, so he could make some fresh dough. Even though I would have to come all the way back across town, I yielded to this request after pausing

a moment for an instantaneous reflection. I knew the man
was tired and had been struggling with his business. Our next
stop was to pick up two clients at their apartment. Although
we had a mutually agreed-upon time, they said they were
doing their laundry and that it wouldn't be done for about 45
minutes. My emotional wounds and pain were triggered. Still,
I took a moment for guidance and reflection. Although not
planning ahead was common for this couple, I was able to
quickly gain a broader perspective with a moment of reflective communion. Who they were had nothing to do with
the emotional reactions going on in me. I was able to calmly
explain that it was courteous to keep agreed-upon schedules
and that I would help them in the future to plan ahead better.
Later, on the way home, we had a flat tire which was very
stressful for me. After the service station attendant changed
the tire, he made an inquiry of me which one of my clients
began answering. I strongly told Sam to get in the car! Af-
terwards, I calmed down and apologized for being abrupt.

Life's journey is not easy. At times it feels like one challenge after another within a larger context of complete chaos.
With our mass media, we can view the external world's
tragedies, scandals, mishaps and messes on a daily basis, and
with a little internal reflection we know the discord that exists
within ourselves. How do we accept the turmoil in life and
still live reasonable lives? As I have illustrated, we must
realize that we belong to a greater organization that is beyond
our human understanding. Yet pursuing this divine mystery is
our greatest gift to ourselves and others and requires a deep
level of faith, acceptance and surrender. Tragedy and suffering are a part of our human condition, perspective and reality
– no matter how we whitewash it. One can reasonably assume that life is meant to be just that way; "a thing is what it
is." However, this can be seen in a new light by first accept-

ing "what is" and then having the faith to move forward with divine guidance as a part of the creation dynamic.

Faith is the acceptance of "what is" with the self-awareness that my life is not totally cut off and separate. The Sacred and Holy are within each individual, moment and experience. When this profoundly simple knowledge and wisdom is grasped, there follows an allowing and yielding to every divine instant with a passion that forbids complacency yet concedes the river will flow as it may. Without personal bias or preference, love is engendered when abundance is seen as accepting all life experiences as valuable. The following Zen story is a shinning light on this human predicament:

A long time ago a monk lived on a hilltop overlooking a fishing village. The monk was the spiritual light of this small settlement. As often happens, a young couple fell madly in love and their passion sparked the seed for a new life. This was completely against the mores and taboos of the people and meant immediate death for any violator. When the young maiden's pregnancy was discovered, the town's elders and people were in an uproar demanding to know the child's father. Since this would mean her lover's death, she said that it was the monk on the hill, knowing that because of his sacred status he would not be harmed. That night the baby was born and in a rage and horror at the law's transgressor, the people gathered with torches, taking the baby up the hill and demanding that the monk rear the child. In response the monk said, "ah so," taking the infant and raising him as his own. Years passed, and the monk suffered the animosity of his people, but took loving care of the baby, helping him to mature and grow into adolescence. Now, the young man's mother became very ill with cancer and lay on her death bed. Not wanting to die with the burden of her sin, she told the people the truth regarding the monk. The townspeople felt great shame and gathered on the top of the hill asking the monk's forgiveness and saying they would now care for the young man. Again, the monk's response was "ah so."

Yielding to "what is" – with a passion that forbids complacency – avows and appreciates God by living in the context of our lives while listening to our heart's insight, wisdom and passion. Surrendering with faith is moving into the unknown while saying yes to all life's experiences knowing that faith and prayer transcend all physical laws without violating them. One need not stand alone in the illusion of separation – together we can all move towards wholeness by consciously allowing a power greater than ourselves an active place within our lives. To be open to this mystery without limits is a constant challenge but our greatest gift to ourselves and others.

The Life Force is: Both Individual and Collective

As discussed in the previous chapter, human beings are being pulled, tugged, and pushed by many external and internal forces. We saw how individual awareness can be influenced by conditioning, habits, emotions, reason, psychological injury, and the sensory limitations of the brain. We know how desire can influence behavior, often in dramatic ways, as in love and religious fanaticism. Consequently, with all these forces impinging on humanity, we can easily conclude that independent choice and free-will – if they exist at all – are severely limited in the truest sense of the words. Yet life fills us with the seductive illusion of free will in our daily lives with thousands of choices: preferences on food, people, entertainment, religions etc., which at the time do not seem affected by the aforementioned human limitations. Nonetheless, true choice can only be a function of an open, non-reactive, unencumbered, present, and self-aware human being.

Mystics describe a unified oneness behind everyday reality which implies that humanity lives on many levels of reality from simple conditioned responses to the experience and knowing of the unity in all existence. This grander perspective and experience of the mystics can transform patterned lives into a more whole and complete individual. These transformations can be a total revamping of the personality or, as is the case of most of the stories in the book, enough of a change to move a person on the path towards wholeness.

As described earlier, one's perspective and life choices are usually limited by all the factors inherent to our species, yet individuals do transcend these limitations, acquiring a more collective view as did the mystics. Unfortunately, most people live in closed or partially closed psychological systems and are truly stuck in the core patterns of their lives.

Similarly, most religions and spiritual paths are closed systems and are based on a tradition of past beliefs which forces spirituality to be static rather than dynamic. When theology becomes dogmatic, rigid or closed in any way, new perspectives and personal transformation are daunted. Nonetheless, our spiritual nature is amazingly strong. Its challenge is to work within closed systems, either organizational or personal.

Within a closed system it is difficult to get perspective. We live in a house of mirrors that reflect back our own images and beliefs, and we affiliate with individuals and organizations that overtly and unconsciously reinforce them. This conformity within individuals and organizations creates a false sense of security and comfort but diminishes the dynamic quality of life and our spiritual natures. Openness to the Divine dwindles as we become more sure that our knowledge and perspective are correct. Joseph Campbell said, "Those that think they know – don't know and those that know they don't know really know." I have heard humility defined as being teachable, which reminds me of the Presbyterian minister who went to visit a Zen master to learn more about his teachings. Upon his arrival, he was invited to join the master for tea. After their initial greeting, the master began pouring the minister a cup of tea until his cup was overflowing. The minister noticing what was happening and said, "my cup is overflowing – my cup is overflowing." The Zen master replied, "It is hard to add to a cup that is already full."

Inherent in all organizations and individuals are contradictions, paradoxes, and beliefs that need thorough and continued examination. To know that even with the strongest convictions, one doesn't have all the answers to life's deepest mysteries requires a sincere openness and searching for answers that can shake our spiritual foundation and traditions; to do otherwise is to be lost in a mirror of self-affirming and self-generated beliefs. If you're not continually questioning what you believe, you live in a closed system!

Individuals cannot be fully aware of all the forces in life! This truth elucidates our personal powerlessness and our lack of control over much of our lives. Nonetheless, the mystical experience of unity behind everything ensures the possibility of wholeness as part of our human inheritance since unity must exist everywhere even within the illusion of being separate. The paradox of individuality and yet the possibility of wholeness in unity is a quintessential problem of human existence. To have the spiritual realms of unity be a conscious part of our daily human existence requires a continual commitment to humility. Even at the most aware and conscious state, humility reminds us that our actual resources are limited which can engender an **allowing** and **yielding** to the Other, the divine aspect of individuality. This opens us to be imbued with wisdom and direction.

Personality-Ego, the "I" of experience, is like a raft on life's turbulent ocean being bounced around by ever shifting waves and currents. In the middle of the Big Unconscious Ocean we individually float on our human raft. Just imagine your feeling and thoughts on a actual raft in the middle of the Pacific Ocean. Help!!! Survival, desires, and obligations can become life's foreground, virtually eliminating any quest for wholeness. Yet unity and wholeness calls to us, beckoning with its ambiance of peace, balance and serenity to search for its stable ground. Are we listening? How distracted are we? Seek the kingdom of heaven first and all else will be given onto you. The kingdom of heaven is not open to personal, religious, or theological definition. It must be experienced.

In life, the personality's fuel is self-will. When misdirected, it places demands, images, beliefs and perspectives on the everyday world, attempting to force complete domain over reality. Turmoil often signals that the personality's fuel is being inappropriately used foregoing the serenity and harmony of Unity's bigger picture. Self-will can be used either negatively or positively. The mature personality uses self-will to balance the needs of the individual with the needs of the whole. The mature personality grows in the ability to include Unity in all thoughts and actions ranging from compassionate unconditional love to the hard realities of tough love. Unity exists even within the tragedies of life, even though this can be hard to fathom when the personality is self-contained in its own mirrored creations. For example the recent movie, Titanic, illustrates the horror that life events can have on individuals, and the complete vulnerability of human life. Still, the harmony of something greater than oneself can be seen in the musicians who play on within ever growing circles of apparent chaos.

Although there is unity in all creation, responsibility for one's life rests with the individual. This is an awesome task requiring a commitment to ever increasing self-awareness. Again, unity must be within every separate individual and thing in order for it to exist at all. Paradoxically what seems only external and separate must somehow be contained within all of creation. The external and internal are equally sides of the same coin, the coin of manifestation and Unity. As self-awareness and expanded states of consciousness grow, one begins to comprehend that ultimate mystery is *unknowable*. Dimly felt or fully recognized, this knowledge leads to either ever increasing reliance on separateness or to a deeper surrendering and yielding. This is true in the secular as well as the religious world. As Bella Karish said, "You can believe yourself to be spiritual and shout it from the housetops and it might not mean a thing."

Throughout our history, individuals have chosen many different life paths. Ascetics have turned away from the secular world to devote themselves completely to divine work as they see it. Others have pursued gratification and fulfillment of individual needs. Ultimately, who can say how an individual should conduct his life, except where human morals are concerned. To hurt others for self-aggrandizement is simply wrong, and yet, most of us have to some extent strayed in that direction. In fact, it seems inevitable when conflicting needs arise between two or more individuals, groups or nations. Still if we believe that behind separateness is a unifying force, then this coalescing energy can be available anytime.

Many believe and experience this unity through heart-level awareness, the consciousness of unconditional love and harmony. This expanded way of knowing and perceiving shifts one's awareness and can bring harmony even in the midst of chaos. Unfortunately, chaos in the external lives of individuals, corporations and nations is not always resolvable. For instance, should the Titanic and/or any other horrific human tragedies be prevented by divine intervention? One can easily and immediately say Yes. Divine intervention is alive in its many forms: as illustrated by the stories in this book, life's daily miracles, and the direct application of divinity in Jesus Christ and other spiritual leaders. Nonetheless, we know that Christ's own horrific death wasn't prevented either by himself or the Godhead so the destiny of the scriptures could be fulfilled and made whole. Jung says that inherent in the human psyche is the movement toward wholeness, the unfoldment and awareness of our complete being in all its potential.

This implies that chaos, the pain in individual life and the horror in collective life play a part in the human awareness of Unity.

If Christ, the Man-God, truly had free will with the ability to exclude deterministic forces and yet chose destiny, then a communion through surrender and alignment with the Godhead took place – "your will and mine". As we become more aware and conscious, personal choices seem less relevant in contrast to the backdrop of the All in All. Still, in the everyday world we must make choices which give birth to life experiences. Out of experience, one can find a personal myth, your own life purpose. This can lead to a differentiated individual, true to himself and still true to Unity. As we become conscious of all the opposing forces and structures within ourselves, Jung says that there is a "transcendent function" that unites and harmonizes the polarities in the individual and perhaps the collective life as well.

The mystics say that unity already exists. To realize this truth one needs to blend and fuse completely with the ambiance of this divine fragrance, breathing into every cell, psychological function and spiritual dimension the wisdom of being fully whole and yet fully separate. Few realize this truth completely, but to act and live life as if it were true will transform any person., for to do so allows the divine aspect of ourselves within every moment of our life. THIS IS A GREAT CHALLENGE – one that requires a faith large enough to move a mountain and big enough to accept the horror in life while seeing the beauty. Nonetheless, one must realize that life continues to grind away at itself on the path toward the conscious awareness of unity – of the separate and the one. Only the conscious, aware individual can realize the two in the one, thus becoming God's realized masterpiece.

Ralph Waldo Trine

In Tune With the Infinite
(or Fullness of Peace, Power and Plenty)

The Supreme Fact of Human Life

From the great central fact of the universe in regard to which we have agreed, namely, this Spirit of Infinite Life that is back of all and from which all comes, we are led to inquire as to what is the great central fact in human life. From what has gone before, the question almost answers itself.

The great central fact in human life, in your life and in mine, is the coming into a conscious, vital realization of our oneness with this Infinite Life, and the opening of ourselves fully to this divine inflow. This is the great central fact in human life, for in this all else is included, all else follows in its train. In just the degree that we come into a conscious realization of our oneness with the Infinite Life, and open ourselves to this divine inflow, do we actualize in ourselves the qualities and powers of the Infinite Life.

And what does this mean? It means simply this: that we are recognizing our true identity, that we are bringing our lives into harmony with the same great laws and forces, and so opening ourselves to the same great inspirations, as have all the prophets, seers, sages, and saviours in the world's history, all men of truly great and mighty power. For in the degree that we come into this realization and connect ourselves with this Infinite Source, do we make it possible for the higher powers to play, to work, to manifest through us.

We can keep closed to this divine inflow, to these higher forces and powers, through ignorance, as most of us do, and thus hinder or even prevent their manifesting through us. Or we can intentionally close ourselves to their operations and thus deprive ourselves of the powers to which, by the very nature of our being, we are rightful heirs. On the other hand, we can come into so vital a realization of the oneness of our real selves with this Infinite Life, and can open ourselves so fully to the incoming of this divine inflow, and so to the operation of these higher forces, inspirations, and powers, that we can indeed and in truth become what we may well term, God-men.

And what is a God-man? One in whom the powers of God are manifesting, though yet a man. No one can set limitations to a man or a woman of this type; for the only limitations he or she can have are those set by the self. Ignorance is the most potent factor in setting limitations to the majority of mankind; and so the great majority of people continue to live their little, dwarfed, and stunted lives simply by virtue of the fact that they do not realize the larger life to which they are heirs. They have never as yet come into a knowledge of the real identity of their true selves.

Mankind has not yet realized that the real self is one with the life of God. Through its ignorance it has never yet opened itself to the divine inflow, and so has never made itself a channel through which the infinite powers and forces can manifest. When we know ourselves merely as men, we live accordingly, and have merely the powers of men. When we come into the realization of the fact that we are God-men, then again we live accordingly, and have the powers of God-men. *In the degree that we open ourselves to this divine inflow are we changed from mere men into God-men.*

A friend has a beautiful lotus pond. A natural basin on his estate – his farm as he always calls it – is supplied with water from a reservoir in the foothills some distance away. A gate regulates the flow of the water from the main that conducts it from the reservoir to the pond. It is a spot of transcendent beauty. There, through the days of the perfect summer weather, the lotus flowers lie full blown upon the surface of the clear, transparent water. The June roses and other wild flowers are continually blooming upon its banks. The birds come here to drink and to bathe, and from early until late one can hear the melody of their song. The bees are continually at work in this garden of wild flowers. A beautiful grove, in which many kinds of wild berries and many varieties of brakes and ferns grow, stretches back of the pond as far as the eye can reach.

Our friend is a man, nay more, a God-man, a lover of his kind, and as a consequence no notice bearing such words as "Private grounds, no trespassing allowed," or "Trespassers will be prosecuted," stands on his estate. But at the end of a beautiful by-way that leads through the wildwood up to this enchanting spot, stands a notice bearing the words "All are welcome to the Lotus Pond." All love our friend. Why? They can't help it. He so loves them, and what is his is theirs.

Here one may often find merry groups of children at play. Here many times tired and weary looking men and women come, and somehow, when they go their faces wear a different expression, – the burden seems to be lifted; and now and then I have heard them when leaving, sometimes in a faint murmur, as if uttering a benediction, say, "God bless our brother-friend." Many speak of this spot as the Garden of God. My friend calls it his Soul Garden, and he spends many hours in quiet here. Often have I seen him after the others have gone, walking to and fro, or sitting quietly in the clear moonlight on an old rustic bench, drinking in the perfume of the wild flowers. He is a man of a beautifully simple nature. He says that here the real things of life come to him, and that here his greatest and most successful plans, many times as by a flash of inspiration, suggest themselves to him.

Everything in the immediate vicinity seems to breathe a spirit of kindliness, comfort, goodwill, and good cheer. The very cattle and sheep as they come to the old stone-fence at the edge of the grove and look across to this beautiful spot seem, indeed, to get the same enjoyment that the people are getting. They seem almost to smile in the realization of their contentment and enjoyment; or perhaps it seems so to the looker-on, because he can scarcely help smiling as he seems the manifested evidence of their contentment and pleasure.

The gate of the pond is always open wide enough to admit a supply of water so abundant that it continually overflows a quantity sufficient to feed a stream that runs through the fields below, giving the pure mountain water in drink to the cattle and flocks that are grazing there. The stream then flows on through the neighbors' fields.

Not long ago our friend was absent for a year. He rented his estate during his absence to a man who, as the world goes, was of a very "practical" turn of mind. He had no time for anything that did not bring him direct "practical" returns. The gate connecting the reservoir with the lotus pond was shut down, and no longer had the crystal mountain water the opportunity to feed and overflow it. The notice of our friend, "All are welcome to the Lotus Pond," was removed, and no longer were the gay companies of children and of men and women seen at the pond. A great change came over everything. On account of the lack of the life-giving water the flowers in the pond wilted, and their long stems lay stretched upon the mud in the bottom. The fish that formerly swam in its clear water soon died and gave an offensive odor to all who came near. The flowers no longer bloomed on its banks. The birds no longer came to drink and to bathe. No longer was heard the hum of the bees; and more, the stream that ran through the fields below dried up, so that the cattle and the flocks no longer got their supply of clear mountain water.

The difference between the spot now and the lotus pond when our friend gave it his careful attention was caused, as we readily see, by the shutting of the gate to the pond, thus preventing the water from the reservoir in the hills which was the source of its life, from entering it. And when this, the source of its life, was shut off, not only was the appearance of the lotus pond entirely changed, but the surrounding fields were deprived of the stream to whose banks the flocks and cattle came for drink.

In this do we not see a complete parallel so far as human life is concerned? In the degree that we recognize our oneness, our connection with the Infinite Spirit which is the life of all, and in the degree that we open ourselves to this divine inflow, do we come into harmony with the highest, the most powerful, and the most beautiful everywhere. And in the degree that we do this do we overflow, so that all who come in contact with us receive the effects of this realization on our part. This is the lotus pond of our friend, he who is in love with all that is truest and best in the universe. And in the degree that we fail to recognize our oneness with this Infinite Source, and so close, shut ourselves to this divine inflow, do we come into that state where there seems to be with us nothing of good, nothing of beauty, nothing of power; and when this is true, those who come in contact with us receive not good, but harm. This is the spot of the lotus pond while the farm was in the hands of a renter.

There is this difference between the lotus pond and your life and mine. It has no power in itself of opening the gate to the inflow of the water from the reservoir which is its source. In regard to this it is helpless and dependent upon an outside agency. You and I have the power, the power within us, to open or to close ourselves to this divine inflow exactly as we choose. This we have through the power of mind, through the operation of thought.

There is the soul life, direct from God. This it is that relates us to the Infinite. There is, then, the physical life. This it is that relates us to the material universe about us. The thought life connects the one with the other. It is this that plays between the two.

INDEX

235

Author Information

Edward L. Walsh has been a licensed psychotherapist for over twenty years. He received his Masters Degree in Counseling from California State University Long Beach in the late 70's. As a psychotherapist, he had worked at a number community counseling agency before establishing a private practice. He has always sought training and experiences that would better his own life and his skills as a psychotherapist.

Born with cerebral palsy, Ed Walsh struggled to cope with society's prejudices, his father's alcoholism, and the effects it had on his family. Being raised a Catholic gave him a strong connection to the mysteries of the spirit, but never fulfilled his deeper longings for spiritual understanding. In 1980, he attended Brugh Joy's foundational conference in Lucerne Valley. This was a profound opening that lead to the exploration of many spiritual traditions and to many experiential awakenings.

Ed Walsh is an accomplished lecturer and storyteller.

Order Form

Please send more information on:

Workshops___, Mailing Lists____, Lectures_____

Name:_____

Address:_____

City:_____State:_____Zip:_____

e-mail address:_____

Sales tax: Please add 7.75 per cent for products shipped to California addresses.

Shipping:

US: $4.00 for one book and $2.00 for each additional book or product.

International: $9.00 for the first book and $5.00 for each additional book or product (estimate)

Send check to:

Open Wings Publishing
P.O. Box 8020
Long Beach, California 90808-0020

Postal orders only

Order Form

Please send more information on:

Workshops___, Mailing Lists____, Lectures_____

Name:_____

Address:_____

City:_____State:_____Zip:_____

e-mail address:_____

Sales tax: Please add 7.75 per cent for products shipped to California addresses.

Shipping:

US: $4.00 for one book and $2.00 for each additional book or product.

International: $9.00 for the first book and $5.00 for each additional book or product (estimate)

Send check to:

Open Wings Publishing
P.O. Box 8020
Long Beach, California 90808-0020

Postal orders only